Encyclopedia of the worlds of Dr Who – A–D

DAVID SAUNDERS is a librarian who has followed *Doctor Who* since its inception. From 1980 to 85 he was Coordinator of the Doctor Who Appreciation Society. He writes regularly for 'Doctor Who Magazine' and has contributed to the science-fiction orientated periodical 'Starburst'.

TONY CLARK is a young, recently-graduated illustrator. This is his first full-length book.

Encyclopedia of the worlds of Dr Who – A–D

By arrangement with BBC Books, a division of BBC Enterprises Ltd. DOCTOR WHO is a registered trade mark of the British Broadcasting Corporation.

KNIGHT BOOKS
Hodder and Stoughton

To RDC, HDP and MAS, who have helped to make *this* world much more bearable, this volume is reciprocally and respectfully dedicated.

Text copyright © David Saunders, 1987
Illustrations copyright © Tony Clark, 1987

First published in Great Britain in 1987 by Piccadilly Press

Knight Edition published 1988

British Library C.I.P.

Saunders, David
Encyclopedia of the worlds of Dr. Who. A–D
1. Children's television drama series in English: Doctor Who
I. Title II. Clark, Tony
791.45'72

ISBN 0-340-42842-2

The characters and situations in this book are entirely imaginary and bear no relation to any real person or actual happening

This book is sold subject to the condition that it shall not, by way of trade or otherwise, be lent, re-sold, hired out or otherwise circulated without the publisher's prior consent in any form of binding or cover other than that in which it is published and without a similar condition including this condition being imposed on the subsequent purchaser.

No part of this publication may be reproduced or transmitted in any form or by any means, electronically or mechanically, including photocopying, recording or any information storage or retrieval system, without either the prior permission in writing from the publisher or a licence, permitting restricted copying. In the United Kingdom such licences are issued by the Copyright Licensing Agency, 33–34 Alfred Place, London WC1E 7DP.

Printed and bound in Great Britain for Hodder and Stoughton Paperbacks, a division of Hodder and Stoughton Limited, Mill Road, Dunton Green, Sevenoaks, Kent TN13 2YA (Editorial Office: 47 Bedford Square, London WC1B 3DP) by Cox and Wyman Limited, Reading, Berks. Photoset by Rowland Phototypesetting Limited, Bury St Edmunds, Suffolk.

FOREWORD

On 23rd November 1963 I fidgeted and waited impatiently as the News over-ran with coverage of the developments since the Kennedy assassination of the previous day. This delayed the start of the new tea-time serial on BBC television and, as it was to be one with a science fiction theme, I was all the more impatient for it to begin. Once it did start, I was spellbound for twenty-five minutes and when it ended felt that a week was far too long to wait to see what was going to happen in the next Saturday's instalment. Thus began my association with the programme which was to become a British television institution and with a character destined to join such legends as Tarzan, Billy Bunter and Sherlock Holmes in the realms of British fiction. Of all the stories transmitted in nearly a quarter of a century that first episode of *Doctor Who* is still my personal favourite and sums up the personal 'magic' which both epitomises the series for me and holds the ingredients which have kept me an addict to it throughout its long television history.

Little did I know on that dark evening back in 1963 that in 1976 and three Doctors and fifteen companions later a fan-following for the programme would culminate in the founding of the Doctor Who Appreciation Society of which I would become the central organiser for five years (from September 1980 to August 1985) and during which time it would fall to me to spearhead the campaign to combat its threatened cancellation at the whim of the Controller of Programmes. Nor did I ever dream that I would be fortunate enough to come face-to-face with five of the six embodiments of my boyhood hero, particularly my personal favourite, the Second Doctor, Patrick Troughton.

So much knowledge about the series did I glean during my time as Coordinator of the Society that I decided that it must be passed on to other followers of the programme and, thanks to the interest of Piccadilly Press and some thirty months of further research and writing, here is published the reference collection of facts about the series. I hope that perusers of it will enjoy it as much as I have enjoyed compiling it.

I have attempted to make an entry for every named character, planet, process, vehicle, piece of equipment etc in the Doctor's experience in his first six incarnations. The last volume of the encyclopedia will include listings of production details and appendices of offshoots and extensions of the series. No work on this scale can claim to be 100% accurate, even though meticulously prepared and checked, and thus the occasional omission or error may occur. I should like to hear of any examples of either so that adjustments can be made in any further editions.

The entries are in alphabetical order with abbreviations, formulae, vehicle/vessel codes etc given at the beginning of each letter of the alphabet. For characters the entry is made under the second name where known or the forename if the surname is unknown. The exception to this is that entries for companions are all consistently under the name by which they were best known since several of them e.g. Polly, Katarina, Adric never had any other name established for them. For characters that acted deceptively the main entry is made under the actual name rather than the false one e.g. Azmael, Taren Capel and Bennett not Edgeworth, Dask and Koquillian. In the historical stories I take no responsibility for any liberties that writers have taken with facts; the entries that appear herein relate to how events were presented on the television screen! Justification for comments, assumptions and conclusions in the text is made by including the BBC production code for the appropriate story in brackets. To help identify the stories, a season table is included at the beginning of the work, together with the number of episodes per story which were broadcast. The list is in transmission order with the coding letters given before it. At the end of each of the alphabetical volumes is an artiste appendix which lists as many of the actors and actresses who took part in the series as can be established. Not all characters can be listed here as some do not actually appear in a story, are dead before it begins or were played by untraced extras.

In my researches and efforts on this project I have been particularly grateful for the cooperation, assistance, advice and encouragement of Gary Russell, John Nathan-Turner, Deanne Holding and Brenda Gardner as well as for the help of John Ainsworth, Dave Auger, Terrance Dicks, Chris Dunk, Andy Grant, Mary Healey, Lai-Wan Chiu, Richard Landen, Peter Lovelady, Dominic May, David Owen, David Richardson, Nigel Robinson, Michael Smallman and Jan Vincent-Rudzki, not forgetting anyone who has ever contributed to either the DWAS Reference Department or the CMS Space and Time series and especially, for his enthusiasm and inspiration, to my colleague Tony Clark.

DAVID SAUNDERS
July 1987

STORY TABLE

FIRST DOCTOR (1963–1966)

FIRST SEASON

4	A	The Tribe of Gum (aka An Unearthly Child)
7	B	The Daleks (aka The Dead Planet)
2	C	The Edge of Destruction
7	D	Marco Polo
6	E	The Keys of Marinus
4	F	The Aztecs
6	G	The Sensorites
6	H	The Reign of Terror

SECOND SEASON

3	J	Planet of Giants
6	K	The Dalek Invasion of Earth
2	L	The Rescue
4	M	The Romans
6	N	The Web Planet
4	P	The Crusade
4	Q	The Space Museum
6	R	The Chase
4	S	The Time Meddler

THIRD SEASON

4	T	Galaxy Four
1	T/A	Mission to the Unknown
4	U	The Myth Makers
12	V	The Dalek Master Plan
4	W	The Massacre
4	X	The Ark
4	Y	The Celestial Toymaker
4	Z	The Gunfighters
4	AA	The Savages
4	BB	The War Machines

FOURTH SEASON

| 4 CC | The Smugglers |
| 4 DD | The Tenth Planet |

SECOND DOCTOR (1966–1969)

6 EE	The Power of the Daleks
4 FF	The Highlanders
4 GG	The Underwater Menace
4 HH	The Moonbase
4 JJ	The Macra Terror
6 KK	The Faceless Ones
7 LL	The Evil of the Daleks

FIFTH SEASON

4 MM	The Tomb of the Cybermen
6 NN	The Abominable Snowmen
6 OO	The Ice Warriors
6 PP	The Enemy of the World
6 QQ	The Web of Fear
6 RR	Fury from the Deep
6 SS	The Wheel in Space

SIXTH SEASON

5 TT	The Dominators
5 UU	The Mind Robber
8 VV	The Invasion
4 WW	The Krotons
6 XX	The Seeds of Death
6 YY	The Space Pirates
10 ZZ	The War Games

THIRD DOCTOR (1970–1974)

SEVENTH SEASON

4 AAA	Spearhead from Space
7 BBB	(Doctor Who and) The Silurians
7 CCC	The Ambassadors of Death
7 DDD	Inferno

EIGHTH
SEASON
- 4 EEE   Terror of the Autons
- 6 FFF   The Mind of Evil
- 4 GGG The Claws of Axos
- 6 HHH Colony in Space
- 5 JJJ   The Daemons

NINTH
SEASON
- 4 KKK Day of the Daleks
- 4 MMM The Curse of Peladon
- 6 LLL   The Sea Devils
- 6 NNN The Mutants
- 6 OOO The Time Monster

TENTH
SEASON
- 4 RRR The Three Doctors
- 4 PPP Carnival of Monsters
- 6 QQQ Frontier in Space
- 6 SSS   Planet of the Daleks
- 6 TTT   The Green Death

ELEVENTH
SEASON
- 4 UUU The Time Warrior
- 6 WWW Invasion of the Dinosaurs
- 4 XXX Death to the Daleks
- 6 YYY The Monster of Peladon
- 6 ZZZ Planet of the Spiders

FOURTH DOCTOR (1974–1981)

TWELFTH
SEASON
- 4 4A Robot
- 4 4C The Ark in Space
- 2 4B The Sontaran Experiment
- 6 4E Genesis of the Daleks
- 4 4D Revenge of the Cybermen

THIRTEENTH
SEASON
4	4F	Terror of the Zygons
4	4H	Planet of Evil
4	4G	Pyramids of Mars
4	4J	The Android Invasion
4	4K	The Brain of Morbius
6	4L	The Seeds of Doom

FOURTEENTH
SEASON
4	4M	The Masque of Mandragora
4	4N	The Hand of Fear
4	4P	The Deadly Assassin
4	4Q	The Face of Evil
4	4R	The Robots of Death
6	4S	The Talons of Weng-Chiang

FIFTEENTH
SEASON
4	4V	Horror of Fang Rock
4	4T	The Invisible Enemy
4	4X	Image of the Fendahl
4	4W	The Sunmakers
4	4Y	Underworld
6	4Z	The Invasion of Time

SIXTEENTH
SEASON
4	5A	The Ribos Operation
4	5B	The Pirate Planet
4	5C	The Stones of Blood
4	5D	The Androids of Tara
4	5E	The Power of Kroll
6	5F	The Armageddon Factor

SEVENTEENTH
SEASON
4	5J	Destiny of the Daleks
4	5H	City of Death
4	5G	The Creature from the Pit
4	5K	Nightmare of Eden
4	5L	The Horns of Nimon

EIGHTEENTH
SEASON	4 5N	The Leisure Hive
	4 5P	Meglos
	4 5R	Full Circle
	4 5Q	State of Decay
	4 5S	Warriors' Gate
	4 5T	The Keeper of Traken
	4 5V	Logopolis

FIFTH DOCTOR (1982–1984)

NINETEENTH
SEASON	4 5Z	Castrovalva
	4 5W	Four to Doomsday
	4 5Y	Kinda
	4 5X	The Visitation
	2 6A	Black Orchid
	4 6B	Earthshock
	4 6C	Time-Flight

TWENTIETH
SEASON	4 6E	Arc of Infinity
	4 6D	Snakedance
	4 6F	Mawdryn Undead
	4 6G	Terminus
	4 6H	Enlightenment
	2 6J	The King's Demons

ANNIVERSARY
SPECIAL	1 6K	The Five Doctors

TWENTY-FIRST
SEASON	4 6L	Warriors of the Deep
	2 6M	The Awakening
	4 6N	Frontios
	2 6P	Resurrection of the Daleks
	4 6Q	Planet of Fire
	4 6R	The Caves of Androzani

SIXTH DOCTOR (1984–1986)

	4 6S	The Twin Dilemma

TWENTY-SECOND
SEASON

	2 6T	Attack of the Cybermen
	2 6V	Vengeance on Varos
	2 6X	The Mark of the Rani
	3 6W	The Two Doctors
	2 6Y	Timelash
	2 6Z	Revelation of the Daleks

TWENTY-THIRD
SEASON (the Trial of a Time Lord)

	4 7A	The Mysterious Planet
	4 7B	Mindwarp
	4 7C	Terror of the Vervoids
	2	The Ultimate Foe

Atmospheric Density Jackets

ADJ
Atmospheric Density Jacket – two of them, stored in the TARDIS, were worn by the First Doctor and Ian when they set out to explore Vortis. (N)

APC Net
The Amplified Panatropic Computations Network, part of the Matrix on Gallifrey, is a giant computer which contained the memories of all deceased Time Lords. At the moment of death an electrical scan was made of their brain patterns and millions of impulses were immediately transferred into the Network (4P). Subsequently it was refined so that the experiences of living Time Lords were accessed to the Network via a device placed within the control rooms of their TARDISes (7B).

ABBOT, Tom
The foreman of the company quarry-blasting near Nunton. (4N)

ABLIF
One of the Gallifreyans inhabiting the wilderness beyond the Capitol on the Time Lord planet. His hunting party captured Leela and Rodan when they escaped the Chancellery Guards by fleeing into this wasteland. He was killed in a skirmish with Sontaran Troopers. (4Z)

ABOMINABLE SNOWMEN
See YETI

ABU
The companion whose 'dispersal' by the Krotons was witnessed by the Second Doctor, shortly after the TARDIS materialised on the planet of the Gonds. (WW)

ABYDOS
A rival pleasure planet to Argolis. (5N)

ACADEMIUS STOLARIS
An eminent art gallery on the planet Sirius V mentioned by Romana. (5H)

ACHILLES
A Greek prince and leader of the Myrmidons who, whilst engaged in single combat with Hector of Troy, gained the upper hand and slew his opponent when Hector was distracted by the TARDIS materialising. After the siege of Troy he was killed in revenge by Hector's younger brother, Troilus. (U)

ACOMAT
A Mongol warrior under Tegana's com-

mand who attempted to ambush Marco Polo's caravan. When the attack failed he was killed by the War Lord to cover the latter's involvement in it. (D)

ACTEON GALAXY
The galaxy in which the 'blue planet', Metebelis Three, is to be found. (ZZZ)

ADAM
The name adopted by novelist Nigel Castle when he agreed to travel to 'New Earth' during 'Operation Golden Age'. (WWW)

ADRASTA, Lady
The tyrannical ruler of Chloris, where she held sway because she possessed a monopoly on metal which was scarce upon the planet. She imprisoned the Tythonian Ambassador, in a pit from which he was liberated by the Fourth Doctor, after Erato had killed her. (5G)

ADAMS, Corporal
A UNIT soldier assigned to duty at Devesham. An android duplicate of him, built by Styggron, was encountered by the Fourth Doctor and Sarah-Jane on their unscheduled visit to Oseidon and subsequently used in the Kraals' attempted invasion of Earth. (4K)

ADRIC
Adric was a youthful native of the planet Alzarius and an elite among his fellow Alzarians, even if they believed themselves to be Terradonians. This meant that for his youthful years he was blessed with great intelligence, and especially in the field of

Adric

mathematics, for which he had been awarded a blue star-shaped badge. An orphan, he felt that he had no future on Alzarius or even Terradon after his brother, Varsh, was killed by the Marshmen. He stowed away on the TARDIS so that he could join up with the Fourth Doctor and see the universe.

He was in awe of the distant, alien Fourth Doctor and much happier with the personality of the quieter, kinder fifth incarnation. He saw in the TARDIS crew a replacement for the family he had lost but his awkwardness and sometimes clumsy ways meant that relationships were never easy for him. Impetuously brave (5P, 5Y), he was also gullible (5W) and his youthfulness meant that he also lacked common sense and judgement which sometimes exposed his companions to danger. It was as well that he was able to prove himself mathematically (5V, 5T, 6B) for, as he himself admitted, he was no good with his hands (5W) except in order to pick locks. (5T)

The left-handed Adric, like all Alzarians, had a body with tremendous restorative powers and his wounds and bruises soon healed themselves (5R, 5X). Like most youngsters, he was fond of his food when given the chance to feed himself freely (6A). He died tragically but heroically in an antimatter explosion when he sacrificed himself trying to defuse the cyber-bomb aboard Captain Briggs' freighter, clutching the belt woven from marsh reeds which had been his brother's and was the symbol of what he had so often seemed – an outsider. (6B)

Adric may be gone but he was not forgotten, for Nyssa and Tegan were momentarily fooled by an apparition of him shortly after his death (6C) and the Doctor remembered him as his life ebbed away into his fifth regeneration. (6R)

AENEAS
The cousin of Troilus who, arriving shortly after the end of the siege of Troy, took him and Vicki, now named Cressida, along with him when he set out on his wanderings. (U)

AGAMEMNON
The king of Mycenae and war-leader who led his Spartan troops in the siege of Troy following the abduction of his sister-in-law, Helen. (U)

AGELLA
A member of the Movellan commando squad sent to Skaro when the war between that race and the Daleks reached stalemate. A robot in female form, she was overpowered by her confederate Lan, reprogrammed by Tyssan and then helped the Fourth Doctor overcome her fellow crew members. (5K)

AGGEDOR
The last of a species of beast inhabiting the planet Peladon, which, like an Earth dodo, had achieved legendary status. He was caught on the slopes of Mount Megeshra and trained by the High Priest, Hepesh, for his own purposes, including the slaying of Chancellor Torbis. He subsequently killed Hepesh in retaliation for his cruel treatment by the High Priest (MMM). Fifty years later his image was used by trickery on the part

Aggedor

of Ice Lord Azaxyr to terrify superstitious miners. The real Aggedor was killed in a fatal struggle with the traitor Eckersley. (YYY)

AHMED
The Egyptian servant of Marcus Scarman who was with him when the latter broke into the Black Pyramid in 1911. (4G)

AINU
A bandit of simple nature on the planet Chloris. (5G)

AJACKS
A caste on the planet Pluto, mostly miners who lived mainly in Megropolis Three there in the employ of The Company. (4W)

ALA-EDDIN
The evil bandit leader and assassin mentioned in Ping-Cho's recital to those travelling in Marco Polo's caravan. (D)

ALCOTT, Senator
The delegate from the United States of America to the World Peace Conference who was almost murdered, on the Master's instruction, by Captain Chin Lee. (FFF)

ALDO
A somewhat simplistic and irreverent crew member on Rorvik's ship. He was killed when it exploded. (5S)

ALEXANDER THE GREAT
The Macedonian general whom the Doctor implies he has met. (4A)

ALGOL
The planet where the economy fell into a terrible state because of galloping inflation, as mentioned to Davros by the Fourth Doctor. (5J)

ALLEN
An IMC security guard on Uxarius. He was killed by the Primitives. (HHH)

ALPHA
One of the friendly Daleks impregnated with the 'human factor' who began to question orders from the Black Daleks. (LL)

Alpha Centauri

ALPHA CENTAURI
A hermaphrodite hexapod, meek and almost cowardly by nature, with a long life-span. He acted as Ambassador for the Federation to Peladon and was present on both the Third Doctor's visits to that planet. (MMM, YYY)

ALPHA DELTA SIERRA
The call-sign of the aircraft employed by the Chameleons for their cover at Gatwick Airport. (KK)

ALPHA FOUR
The space beacon which was being wired for an explosion by the space pirates when the TARDIS materialised. (YY)

ALPHA MAJOR
The name of the flying saucer belonging to the Daleks in which Ian and Larry Madison travelled to Bedfordshire from London. (K)

ALTOS
An inhabitant of the planet Marinus, Altos was the suitor of Sabetha, daughter of Arbitan. Despatched by Arbitan to recover the keys, he was mesmerised in the city of Morphoton. When rescued from there by the First Doctor, he accompanied Susan, Ian, Barbara and Sabetha in their quest for the remaining keys. (E)

ALUMET, Mount
The mountains where Ala-eddin had his lair. (D)

ALVIS
An assistant in the Youth Centre on the planet where an Earth colony was ruled by the Macra. (JJ)

ALYDON
One of the Thal group encountered by the First Doctor on his original trip to Skaro. He befriended Susan and left an antidote for the time travellers when they were overcome by radiation sickness. When Temmosus was killed by the Daleks he succeeded him as leader of the group. (B)

ALZARIUS

A planet in E-space on which a Terradonian Star Liner had crashed. Its inhabitants evolved periodically from marsh-spiders through marshmen to humanoids, beginning at the season termed Mistfall. It was from this planet that Adric originated. (5R)

AMAZONIA

An Earthwoman who was the Chairman delegate to the Committee of Assessment on behalf of the Federation to judge whether Peladon should be admitted to that body. Her arrival on Peladon was delayed and, in her absence, the other delegates and King Peladon mistook the Third Doctor for the ambassador and Jo for a princess, a royal observer. (MMM)

AMBOISE, Abbot of

The right-hand man of the Cardinal of Lorraine and one of the agents of Gaspard de Saux-Tavannes, Marshal of France. When Admiral de Coligny escaped death at the hand of his hired killer, Bondot, the Abbot was blamed for the failure of the assassination and killed on the orders of his employer. He was physically identical to the First Doctor. (W)

AMBRIL

The Director of Historical Research on Manussa. (6D)

AMDO

The goddess worshipped by the inhabitants

of Atlantis. The Second Doctor was to be sacrificed to her by Lolem, her High Priest, and escaped when Polly spoke through the mouth of the idol erected to her. (GG)

AMMONIA
The atmosphere in which the Rills exist. (T)

AMSTERDAM
The city in Holland where Omega located the curve in the Arc of Infinity and effected a temporary bonding with the Fifth Doctor. (6E)

AMYAND
One of the inhabitans of Sarn, branded a heretic by Timanov because he refused to believe in Logar. (6Q)

ANAT
The leader of a guerilla task force from the 22nd century who travelled back two centuries to execute Sir Reginald Styles in an attempt to change history so that the Daleks would not become rulers of the Earth in her time. (KKK)

ANATTA
The female chess-player about whom Tegan dreamed when she fell asleep under the wind-chimes on Deva-Loka. (5Y)

ANDERSEN, Hans Christian
The Danish writer of children's stories whom the Doctor mentions he has met. (M)

Anat

ANDOR
The leader of the Sevateem at the time of the Fourth Doctor's second visit to their planet. He was killed in a psychic assault by the Evil One, Xoanon. (4Q)

ANDRED
Commander of the Gallifreyan Chancellery Guard at the time of the Fourth Doctor's second visit there. Believing the Doctor to be a traitor, he participated in an assassination plot against him, but on realising his true intent helped him against the Vardans and

Sontarans. Leela remained on Gallifrey to be with him. (4Z)

ANDREWS, Jim
The duty officer at Heathrow Airport when the TARDIS materialised there in 1982. (6C)

ANDREWS, John
One of the crew of the cargo ship, the S.S. Bernice, kidnapped and stored in the miniscope brought to Inter-Minor by the Lurman Vorg and Shirna. (PPP)

ANDROGUMS
A race of servile aliens with a carnivorous streak. Dastari attempted to turn the Second Doctor into one and temporarily succeeded. (6W)

ANDROIDS
A robotic duplicate of a life form. During their adventures the Doctor and/or his companions have encountered androids on Androzani Minor (6R), Earth (R, 4J, 5X, 6B), Karfel (6Y), Marinus (E), Mechanus (R), Oseidon (4J), Tara (5D) and on a space ship (5W).

ANDROMEDA
The constellation in which are to be found the planets Castrovalva (5Z) and Salostophus (7A). It is also from where Drathro originated (7A). Mavic Chen attended an intergalactic conference there in the year 4000. (V)

The First Doctor With Dracula Android

ANDROMEDA GAMMA EPSILON

The planet from where the Wirrn originated. They fled into space when humans accidentally destroyed their breeding colonies there. (4C)

ANDROZANI

Androzani Major and Minor were two of the five planets in the Sirius system. Major was civilised and heavily industrialised in contrast with Minor, which was largely uninhabited but on which the drug Spectrox could be found in abundance. (6R)

ANETH

A planet 24 hours' journey from Skonnos

which was forced to send periodic tribute of youths and hymetusite to the Skonnon Empire; all of whom were handed over to the Nimon. (5L)

ANICCA
The male chess-player about whom Tegan dreamed when she fell asleep under the wind-chimes on Deva-Loka. (5Y)

ANIMUS
A spider-like entity which controlled the Zarbi on Vortis. It was destroyed by a cell destructor operated by Barbara. (N)

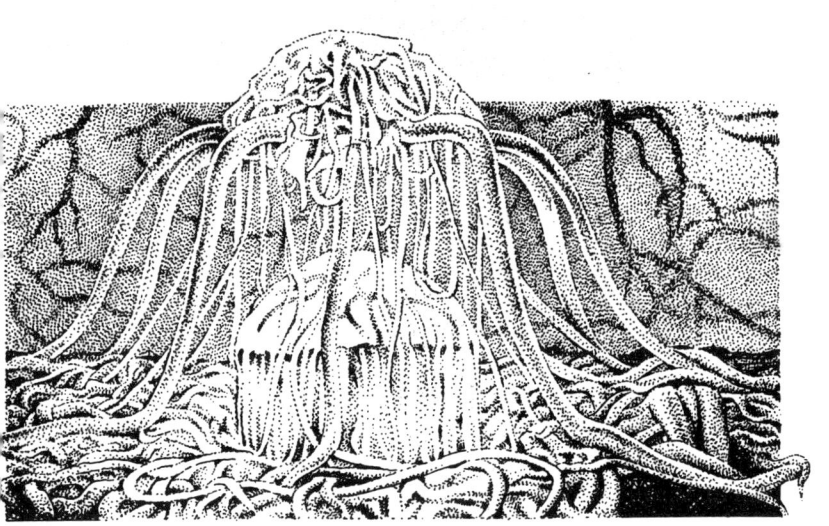

The Animus

ANITA
The Andalusian girl-friend of Oscar Botcherby. (6W)

ANITHON
The 'good' Xeraphin encountered by the Fifth Doctor. (6C)

ANKH
One of the cyborg seers who served the Oracle on the planet which formed round the Minyan spaceship, the P7E. (4Y)

ANNABEL
The ship, under Trask's captaincy, from which Solicitor Gray planned to sell a cargo of prisoners, including Ben and Jamie, into white slavery. (FF)

ANTERIDES
A space region distant from the Artoro Galaxy mentioned by Commander Salamar. (4H)

ANTI-BARYON SHIELDS
An extra part built into the Tachyon Generator by Pangol as part of his preparations for the birth of a new Argolis. (5N)

ANTI-MATTER
The opposite of positive matter. It was from a universe of anti-matter that Omega twice tried to break free (RRR, 6E) and a gateway to which was to be found on the planet Zeta Minor (4H). The fuel on Captain Briggs' freighter was composed of such molecules. This was the reason for the gigantic explosion (wiping out the dinosaurs) which resulted from its collision with Earth in its distant past. Adric was killed in the process. (6B)

ANTODUS
One of the Thal group encountered by the First Doctor on his original trip to Skaro. He accompanied Barbara, Ian, his brother Ganatus, Kristas and Elyon on the rear offensive on the Dalek city. He perished in the cause, committing suicide when he failed to jump a chanced-upon chasm. (B)

ANTON
The pilot of the hovercraft, the crew of which twice attacked the Second Doctor believing him to be Salamander. He was killed in a helicopter explosion over the grounds of Astrid Ferrier's house. (PP)

ARA
The Atlantean girl assigned to Zaroff's staff who helped Polly escape from an operation to turn her into one of the fish people. (GG)

ARAK
The son of Sabor and Neska on the planet Metebelis Three. Together with his brother Tuar he led a revolt against the Eight-Legs who ruled the planet and overthrew them with the help of the Third Doctor and Sarah-Jane. (ZZZ)

ARAK
An inhabitant of Varos and the husband of Etta. (6V)

ARAM
A rebel on the planet Karfel. She was killed by the Borad. (6Y)

ARANA, Dona
The eighty-nine year old blind widow of Don Vincente Arana whose villa was used by Chessene and Stike after she was killed by Shockeye. (6W)

ARAR-JECKS
The inhabitants of Hieradi who hollowed out a huge subterranean city under their planet during their 20-aeon war, mentioned by Turlough. (6N)

ARBITAN
The keeper of the 'Conscience of Marinus'. By placing a forcefield around the TARDIS he ensured a forced search for the four keys of the Conscience by the First Doctor, Susan, Ian and Barbara. Shortly afterwards, he was murdered by the Voord. (E)

ARCALIANS
A chapter of the Time Lords; on ceremonial occasions they wear green robes. (4P)

THE ARC OF INFINITY
A shifting gateway to the dimensions which Omega used to attempt re-entry into the positive universe. (6E)

ARCHER, Colonel
The commanding officer of the squad assigned to guard the Movellan nerve gas cylinders. He was killed on the orders of the Daleks and duplicated. (6P)

ARCHIMANDRITE

The head of the church on Tara who conducted the coronation ceremony for Prince Reynart and subsequently was summoned in the middle of the night by Count Grendel to perform two royal weddings. (5D)

ARCTURUS

A delegate from the planet of the same name sent to the planet Peladon on behalf of the Federation to negotiate that planet's trisilicate deposits in return for admission to that body. He conspired with the High Priest, Hepesh, for the opposite to transpire so that

Arcturus

his planet would, by treaty, gain exclusive rights to the mineral deposits. He was killed by Ssorg (MMM). The planet won the Intergalactic Olympic Games, as mentioned to Davros by the Fourth Doctor (5J) and was an old enemy of Mars. (MMM)

ARDEN
The geologist at Brittanicus base in 3000. He was killed by the Ice Warriors. (OO)

ARETA
The wife of Jondar on Varos. On a whim of Sil's she was almost transmuted into a reptile but was rescued by the Sixth Doctor and her husband. (6V)

ARGOLIS
The planet where The Leisure Hive was situated in 2250. It was almost destroyed in a twenty minute nuclear war between the Argolin and the Foamasi; the Argolin almost died out until their Chairman's wife, Mena, found a method of rejuvenation in Tachyonics. (5N)

ARGONITE
A rare and extremely precious metal mined on the planet Ta by the Issigri Mining Company. It was coveted by the space pirate Caven. (YY)

ARIADNE
The daughter of King Minos of Crete, (who rescued Theseus from the Labyrinth with a ball of twine), whom the Doctor mentions he has met. (5G)

ARIDIUS
A desert-like planet inhabited by creatures who were half-humanoid and half-amphibian and also their sworn enemies the Mirebeasts. (R)

ARIS
The member of the Kinda tribe on Deva-Loka who was temporarily possessed by the Mara during which time he was accidentally injured by Adric in the TSS. (5Y)

THE ARK
The name given by Dodo to the ship in which the survivors from Earth travelled to Refusis II in the 57th segment of time. (X)

ARMAGEDDON CONVENTION
An interplanetary treaty in which the intelligent races of the galaxy attempted to outlaw some of the more lethal weapons, such as cyber-bombs, mentioned by the Doctor. (4D)

Aridians

ARNOLD, Staff Sergeant
A member of Colonel Pemberton's patrol during the Yeti occupation of the London Underground. His mind was controlled by the Great Intelligence. He was killed in the explosion caused by Jamie in order to free the Second Doctor from the Intelligence's mind-siphoning helmet. (QQ)

ARTORO GALAXY
The galaxy in which both Morestria and

Zeta Minor are to be found many light years apart. (4H)

ARTRON ENERGY
A brain impulse, possessed by Time Lords, which is connected with the ability to reason and to calculate. (4P, 5W)

ASCARIS
The mute assassin hired to dispose of Maximus Pettulian in 64 A.D. (M)

ASHBRIDGE
A town on the edge of Oxley Woods in Essex. It was to the cottage hospital there that the Third Doctor was taken. He had been found unconscious next to the TARDIS after landing on Earth to begin his exile. (AAA)

ASHE FAMILY
Robert Ashe was the leader of the colonists on Uxarius against whom the IMC team waged a subversive campaign aimed at forcing them to leave and settle elsewhere. He had a daughter, Mary, who befriended Jo. Robert died heroically in a rocket explosion, trying to lull the miners into believing the colonists had quit the planet by piloting the battered craft single-handedly. (HHH)

ASHTON
A black marketeer at the time of the Dalek Invasion of Earth, who was killed by the Slyther. (K)

ASSISSIUM
A town north of Rome where the First Doc-

tor, Ian, Barbara and Vicki stayed at the villa of Flavius Guiscard in 64 A.D. (M)

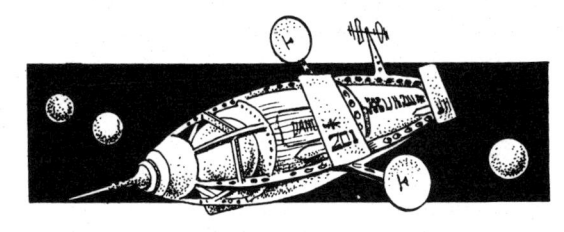

Space Flight To Astra

ASTRA
The planet to which her father was taking Vicki in 2493 following the death of her mother, before he was killed by Bennett. (L)

ASTRA, Princess
The Princess of the planet Atrios. In actuality she was the sixth segment of the Key to

Princess Astra

Time. Once the key had been redispersed she set her mind on marrying her suitor, Surgeon Merak (5F). Romana chose to adopt Astra's features when she regenerated. (5J)

ATLANTIS
The legendary city which sank beneath the sea. Three parts of the city have been known by the Doctor to have met with disaster on separate occasions: that which was terminated by the Daemons as recalled by Azal (JJJ), that which Professor Zaroff maniacally tried to flood (GG) and the part of the Minoan civilisation doomed by the Master. (OOO)

ATRIOS
A planet which at the time of the Fourth Doctor and Romana's materialisation there was engaged in a nuclear war engineered by the Shadow, with its twin, Zeos. (5F)

ATROPINE POISONING
The cause of the deaths of many Sensorites on the Sense-Sphere in the 28th century. It was the result of the introduction by demented Earth astronauts of deadly nightshade into the water supply. (G)

ATTWOOD, Colonel
The commander of the Inverness barracks and superior officer of Lieutenant Algernon Ffinch at the time of Solicitor Gray's attempted white slavery. (FF)

ATZA
One of the Mogarians travelling on the Hyperion III. He was killed by Doland. (7C)

AUDERLEY HOUSE
The government owned residence from which the peace diplomat Sir Reginald Styles worked. It was destroyed by a Dalekanium bomb detonated by the twenty-second century guerilla Shura. (KKK)

AUKON
The name adopted by Science Officer Anthony O'Connor of the Earth spaceship, Hydrax, when he became High Councillor and one of the Three Who Rule on the planet in E-space where the Hydrax was drawn by the Great Vampire. He and his vampiric companions Zargo and Camilla crumbled to dust when the Fourth Doctor successfully destroyed the Great Vampire. (5P)

AUTLOC
The Aztec High Priest of Knowledge who believed Barbara to be the reincarnation of Yetaxa. Enlightened by the time travellers as to the barbaric ways of his people, he left them and went to live in the desert. (F)

AUTONS
Mannikins of plastic controlled by the Nestenes. There are two types: Killer Autons which are humanoid in shape with energy bolt guns concealed within the right hand and Replicas which are intrinsic facsimiles of human subjects. The latter are accurate in every detail, possessing memory traces and

Autloc

Autons

such refined plastic skin that it is almost impossible to distinguish between the original and the impersonation. Killer Autons have appeared on Earth as shop window dummies, 'waxworks' and carnival-headed advertising campaign personnel, whilst Replicas include Channing, Scobie, Channing's secretary, policemen and factory workers. Autons have twice been used to spearhead a Nestene invasion of Earth, on the second occasion in collaboration with the Master. (AAA, EEE)

AVERY, Captain
The deceased captain of the Black Albatross whose treasure was hidden by one of his former crew, the Cornish churchwarden, Joseph Longfoot. (CC)

AVON
The young man who acted as guide for

Steven and Dodo when they were shown around the city of the Elders. (AA)

AXOS

Axos is a single biological entity of planet-sized proportions which can split off sections of itself in the continuing quest for nourishment.

A large chunk of Axos was guided to Earth by the Master, who was imprisoned within it. It landed in the guise of a biological space craft and proceeded to distribute quantities of Axonite to all points of our globe. Axonite is a complex compound which, when 'activated', expands to engulf any source of energy, converting it into the raw foodstuff upon which Axos feeds. In order to ensure worldwide distribution of Axonite the main Axos body changed part of itself into human-

Axos

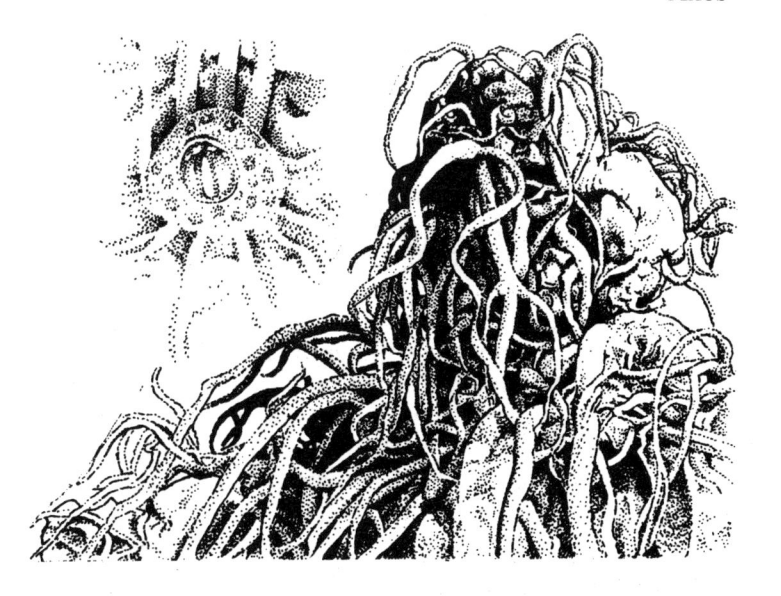

oid form which those who met them believed to be a family of peaceful space travellers. When UNIT fought back against them these golden-skinned creatures were reconverted into a writhing mass of organic life, orange in hue and capable of storing and projecting lethal electrical charges. In an unwilling alliance with the Master, the Third Doctor managed to trap the Axon vessel into a time-loop. (GGG)

AXUS

One of the Gond race enslaved by the Krotons, he had the position of guard-captain and challenged Jamie on his arrival in the Hall of Learning. (WW)

AYDAN

The murderer of Eprin, for which crime Ian was tried in the city of Millenius. When he was about to turn 'Queen's Evidence' at Ian's trial he was killed in the courtroom by his wife, Kala. (E)

AZAL

The last of the Daemons who visited Earth and helped to shape its history. His power was released through psionic science by the Master. When he offered to bequeath this power to and was refused by the Third Doctor, Azal attempted to obliterate him. Confused by Jo's act of self-sacrifice in interposing herself between them, Azal was unable to prevent his own energy from being deflected back at himself and was destroyed. (JJJ)

AZAXYR

An Ice Lord and the commander of a breakaway group of Ice Warriors who were agents of Galaxy Five. With the help of Eckersley he planned to betray the Federation and ship Peladonian trisilicate to their masters. He was killed by being stabbed in a struggle with miners and royal guards whilst threatening Queen Thalira. (YYY)

AZMAEL

The Time Lord friend of the Doctor and President of Jaconda. He committed suicide by attempting a thirteenth regeneration in order to free Jaconda and himself from Mestor's rule. (6S)

AZTECS

The Central American culture in which the First Doctor and his companions lived when they were temporarily separated from the TARDIS by a secret door, after the time machine had materialised in the tomb of Yetaxa. (F)

AZURE

The pleasure planet in the orbit of which a space accident involving the cruise-liner Empress and the privately-owned Hecate took place. Excise officials from the planet were sent to the scene of the occurrence and found that there was also the question of drug smuggling to be investigated. (5L)

BBC-3
The television station which reported on the opening of the Devil's Hump during the festival of Beltane. (JJJ)

BIDS
The British Institute of Druidic Studies of which Leonard de Vries was the leader. (5C)

BOSS
Biomorphic Organisational Systems Supervisor: a computer situated on the top floor of Global Chemicals in Llanfairfach. It was linked to the brain of the company's managing director, Dr Thomas Stevens, whom it controlled. It planned to take over the world by linking itself to every major computer. The Doctor used his Metebelis crystal to break its control over Stevens, who promptly destroyed the machine. (TTT)

BACCU
One of the Guardians travelling towards

Refusis II on The Ark encountered by the First Doctor on his first visit there. (X)

BACON, Sir Francis
A sixteenth century playwright; a conversation between him, Elizabeth I and William Shakespeare was observed by the First Doctor and his companions on the Time-Space Visualiser given to the Doctor by the Xerons. (R)

BAKER
One of Dortmun's resistance fighters in 2164. He helped rescue the First Doctor from the Dalek saucer, Alpha Major, but was subsequently killed by a Dalek patrol. (K)

BAKER, Major
The Security Officer at the Atomic Research Centre on Wenley Moor who was the first to be infected with plague by the Silurians and subsequently died. (BBB)

BALAN
The Dulcian Educator who took two of his students on a survey of the Island of Death. He was killed by a Quark. (TT)

BALARIUM
The yellow gas by which the Fourth Doctor was overcome when he attempted to defraud the Consum bank on Pluto. (4W)

BALATON
The grandfather of Pralix and Mula on Zanak. (5B)

BALAZAR
The 'Reader of the Books' in Marb Station on Ravolox. (7A)

BALDWIN
A member of Sorenson's expedition to Zeta-Minor who was destroyed by the anti-matter creature. (4H)

BANDRAGINUS V
A planet, robbed of its mineral wealth and energy, shrunk and kept in his trophy room by the Captain. (5B)

BANDRIL
The neighbouring planet of Karfel with which the Karfelons traded. (6Y)

BANE
One of Lieutenant Scott's troopers. She was killed by the Cybermen's androids. (6B)

BARBARA
Kidnapped from her own world and time, Barbara Wright was at first angry at, and subsequently tolerant of, the situation into which she and Ian Chesterton had thrust themselves. Barbara and her fellow teacher from Coal Hill School had taken an interest in a strange pupil known to them as Susan Foreman.

Once she and Ian understood the Doctor's reason for taking them with him and his frustration at subsequently being unable to return them to London in 1963, she became a tower of strength to her fellow travellers and,

Barbara

particularly to Susan, a comfort throughout the perils they endured together.

She was possessed of an open mind and evident intelligence and had a very good grounding in history (the subject which she taught) and geography. This was of particular help during the journey to Cathay (D), the enforced stay in Central America (F) and at the time of Robespierre. (H)

She had a compassionate nature which came to the fore in her treatment of the Doctor once Susan had left them (L) and was immediately kind to the orphaned Vicki (also L). She was brave too, as witnessed by her stands against Tloloxl (F) and the

Animus (N) and well able to take care of the amorous advances of Léon Colbert (H) and Nero (M). She could, however, be moody; as in the instance when her suspicions that sabotage was not to blame for the strange events in the ship were proved correct. Whereupon, she sulked until the Doctor came to apologise (C). Wearied by what seemed to be endless travelling, she was the first to realise that she and Ian might be able to return home in the annihilated Daleks' time machine. Prepared to take the risk of miscalculation, she urged her companion to join her in the gamble to return home. They arrived in London but two years later than when they had 'disappeared'. Happy to be home again they knew that the wealth of experience which they had acquired whilst with the Doctor would remain with them always.

BARCLAY

One of the guards at the castle where the Master was confined under Colonel Trenchard's supervision. (LLL)

BARCLAY, Doctor Tom

The Australian physicist and second-in-command of the Snowcap base who helped the First Doctor, Ben and Polly despite the bureaucratic order of the Base Commander, General Cutler. (DD)

BARNES

One of the inmates of the meditation centre in Mummerset who helped the power-seeking Lupton and was left with a nervous breakdown after being possessed by one of the Eight-Legs. (ZZZ)

BARNEY
The supervisor of the Refreshing Department on the planet where an Earth colony was ruled by the Macra. (JJ)

BARNHAM, George
A convict and inmate of Stangmoor Prison. He had his mind cleansed by the Keller Machine which left him with the mentality of a child. He helped the Third Doctor to defeat the Master and was finally killed by him. (FFF)

BARRAS, Paul
A deputy of France in 1794 and one of the conspirators in the plot to depose Robespierre. (H)

BARRINGTON, Major
One of the conditioned British participants in The *War Games* in the World War I zone. (ZZ)

BARTHOLOMEW'S EVE MASSACRE, SAINT
The slaughter of Huguenots by Catholics on the eve of the saint's festival day in Paris on 24th August 1572. (W)

BASS, Tim
A miner in Killingworth in the seventeenth century. He was operated on by the Rani and turned relentlessly aggressive. (6X)

BATES
A semi-cybernised prisoner on Telos who was killed by the Cybermen whilst trying to escape. (6T)

BAX
A member of the Officer Guard Elite on Varos in the Communications Division. (6V)

BAXTER, Chief
The chief engineer in command of the control Gas Rig in the North Sea in the 1970s. (RR)

BAXTER, Ruth
The mutated laboratory assistant to Doland, who was killed by the Vervoids. (7C)

THE BEATLES
The 1960s pop group from Liverpool which the First Doctor and his companions observed singing their hit song 'Ticket to Ride' on the Time-Space Visualiser given to the Doctor by the Xerons. (R)

BEAUS
One of the delegates to the Daleks when they formulated their Master Plan on Kembel. (T/A, V)

BEAVIS, Doctor
The visiting surgeon to Ashbridge Cottage Hospital whose clothes and car were 'bor-

Beaus

rowed' by the newly-regenerated Third Doctor so that he could find his TARDIS. (AAA)

BECKET, Sam
The Australian head technician and number 6 on the Moonbase in 2070. (HH)

BEDE, The Venerable
The Anglo-Saxon theologian, historian and chronologist whom the Doctor mentions he has met. (4S)

BELL, Corporal
A UNIT lady soldier who acted as secretary and personal assistant to the Brigadier during the World Peace Conference (FFF) and the Ministry of Defence inspection. (GGG)

BELL, Alexander Graham
The inventor of the telephone whom the Doctor mentions he has met. (4J)

BELLAL
An Exxilon who befriended the Third Doctor and Sarah-Jane and helped them against the Daleks. (XXX)

BELL PLANTS
Lush but carnivorous vegetation on the planet Tigella. (5Q)

BELTANE
The greatest occult festival of the year bar Hallowe'en, celebrated on April 30th. It was at midnight on Beltane that Professor Horner planned to open up the barrow nicknamed the Devil's Hump outside the village of Devil's End. (JJJ)

BEN
Ben Jackson was tough, resourceful and, like Dodo, a true Cockney. Raised in a large family, he gained his independence at a very early age. He left school in his early teens and was apprenticed to an electrician before he decided to fulfil the popular youngster dream of running away to sea.

He opted for life in the Merchant Navy and it was while he was on shore leave in London that he chanced to meet Polly at a fashionable nightspot, 'The Inferno'. Their paths crossed with that of Dodo, who soon introduced the pair of them to the First Doctor.

After both of them had assisted the Doctor

Corporal Bell   Ben

in defeating the computer WOTAN, Ben and Polly went to the Doctor's TARDIS to return the key which had fallen from a pocket in his cloak. Not knowing that they had come aboard, the Doctor dematerialised the ship and all three of them were soon on course for eighteenth century Cornwall. (BB)

Ben was a naturally loyal person and it came as something of a shock that he seemingly betrayed the Doctor in their encounter with the Macra; however he was acting under the influence of a gas produced by those creatures. (JJ)

Some eight journeys after he had boarded the TARDIS and following the routing of the plans of the Chameleons (KK), Ben took his leave of the Doctor and Jamie at Gatwick

Airport. Polly left at the same time which was, coincidentally, on the same day as their journeying had begun, 20th July 1966. There was little doubt that Ben's destiny was to remain linked with hers after their travels with the Doctor ceased.

BEN
The principal keeper of the Fang Rock lighthouse. He was killed by a Rutan. (4V)

BEN DAHEER
The trader in Jaffa from whom the First Doctor 'borrowed' appropriate clothing for Vicki and himself. (P)

BENIK
The sadistic and unpleasant Deputy Director of the Kanowa Research Centre. (PP)

BENNETT
A killer who had murdered the crew of his space craft, including Vicki's father, and then tried to cover this by attempting the genocide of the inhabitants of the planet Dido. Posing as Koquillian, he befriended and intimidated Vicki. He died when, on catching sight of some surviving Didonians, he overbalanced over a cliff top. (L)

BENNETT, Jarvis
The Controller of the *Wheel in Space*. He was killed by a Cyberman. (SS)

BENOIT, Roger
A French scientist based on the Moonbase of

which he was the second-in-command to Hobson. (HH)

BENSON, Joe
The English physicist and number 9 on the Moonbase in 2070. (HH)

BENTON, Corporal/Sergeant/RSM
A member of UNIT whom the Doctor first encountered as a plainclothes man during the struggle against the Cybermen in London in 1975 (VV). When this occurred he was a corporal but by the time of General Carrington's plot against the ambassadors from Mars (CCC) he had become a sergeant. He remained at this rank throughout the time of the Third Doctor's exile and subsequent adventures on Earth. It was shortly after the Doctor's third regeneration that he was promoted to Warrant Officer. (4A)

Sergeant Benton And Platoon Under Leader Benton

Throughout his association with the Doctor he remained steadfast and unswervingly loyal to him. He never had the opportunity to enter the TARDIS until an attack by the Gell-guards forced him, along with the Third Doctor and Jo, to take refuge there. His only trip away from Earth was to Omega's realm of anti-matter during the same adventure. (RRR)

He had a counterpart on the parallel Earth visited by the Third Doctor (DDD); an unpleasant bully with the rank of Platoon Under Leader, who became infected by the effects of Stahlman's gas and degenerated into a Primord. The Kraals also built an android duplicate of him (4J). Despite being one of the Doctor's close friends, Benton suffered a unique fate when the effects of the Crystal of Kronos temporarily transformed him back into a baby. (OOO)

He reportedly, according to the Brigadier, left UNIT to become a second-hand car salesman, but this may be a figment of the Brigadier's memory, caused by his temporary breakdown. (6F)

BERESFORD, Major

The commanding officer of UNIT in the absence of the Brigadier at the time of the attempted invasion of Earth by the Krynoid. (4L)

BERGER

The First Officer on the freighter commanded by Captain Briggs. (6B)

BERNALIUM

A substance essential to the functioning of

the laser on the *Wheel in Space*. Most of the supply stored there was consumed by cybermats. (SS)

S.S. BERNICE
The cargo ship kidnapped from the Indian Ocean in 1926 and stored in a time-loop in the miniscope brought to Inter-Minor by the Lurman Vorg and Shirna. (PPP)

BESSIE
The Edwardian roadster which the Brigadier arranged to be acquired for the use of the Third Doctor as part of the incentive for him to spend his exile working as Scientific Advisor to UNIT. She made her debut in *The Silurians*. The Third Doctor 'improved' her engine workings so that she could travel at great speeds, though her occupants were protected by inertia absorption (OOO). She was fitted with a remote control device (JJJ) and an anti-theft mechanism which caused would-be thieves to be magnetised to her (CCC) when switched on. While in the possession of the Third Doctor she travelled widely; she was also transported into a parallel Earth world (DDD), to Omega's domain of antimatter (RRR) and even to Gallifrey. (6K)

Her driver was mostly the Doctor in his third incarnation – the Fourth Doctor drove her once (4A) – but she was on occasion driven by others of the Doctor's acquaintance: the Brigadier (CCC and ZZZ), Liz Shaw (CCC), Harry Sullivan (4A) and Sergeant Benton (ZZZ). It is implied that Captain Yates drove her from the heat barrier back to the 'Cloven Hoof' during *The Daemons*. In that same story the Master

Bessie

attempted to steal her to make his getaway but was thwarted by the Doctor's use of the remote control device.

She was painted yellow in colour and her number plate was WHO 1.

BETA
One of the friendly Daleks impregnated with the 'human factor' who began to question orders from the Black Daleks. (LL)

BETA
The Controller of Science among the Gond people. (WW)

BETA DART
The spaceship piloted by, among others, Dervish. (YY)

BETA TWO
A planet in the Perugellis Sector and the destination of the Earth exploration vessel Hydrax which en route there vanished into E-space. (5P)

BETELGUESE
The planet which came second in the Intergalactic Olympic Games, as mentioned to Davros by the Fourth Doctor. (5J)

BETTAN
An aide to the Thal Minister who led an attack on the Kaled Bunker and entombed Davros and the Daleks there. (4E)

BETTS, Private
A UNIT soldier on duty at Llanfairfach at the time of *The Green Death*. (TTT)

BI-AL FOUNDATION
A hospital space-station on asteroid K.4067 near the moon Titan. One of its staff, Professor Marius, helped the Fourth Doctor, Leela and K-9 defeat the Nucleus of the Swarm there in the year 5000. (4T)

BIGON
The Athenian philosopher collected by Monarch and reduced to silicon chips, which were used to motivate an android body. (5W)

Bigon

BILL
One of the sewer surveyors taken prisoner and cybernised by the Cybermen. (6T)

BILTON, Andrew
The First Officer of Concorde Golf Alpha Charlie. (6C)

BINDING ENERGY

The means by which the Nimon remained alive. On every planet they overran they ingested its binding energy until it was sucked dry. (5L)

BINRO

The inhabitant of Ribos who had divined that his planet moved round its sun, for which he had been branded Binro the Heretic by an unbelieving world. He befriended Unstoffe and was killed protecting him from one of the Levithian guards of the Graff Vynda-K. (5A)

BIRASTROP

The animal, the lungs of which were given to the Morbius-monster by Mehendri Solon. (4K)

BIRCH

The manservant of Squire Edwards. (CC)

BIROC

A Tharil enslaved as navigator on Rorvik's ship in E-space. Having escaped, he set about freeing the rest of his race and Romana, together with K-9 Mk. II, stayed to help him. (5S)

BISHAM

An exec. grade and rebel encountered by the Fourth Doctor on Pluto. (4W)

BLACK ALBATROSS

The ship captained by the pirate Samuel

Pike. Its former master, the late Captain Avery, had entrusted his treasure to his then crew-mate Joseph Longfoot. (CC)

BLACK GUARDIAN

The Guardian of Darkness, one of the most powerful beings in the cosmos and the antithesis to the White Guardian. He sought to take the Key to Time for his own (5F) and when thwarted by the Doctor he vowed revenge which he tried to exact through the services of Turlough (6F, 6G) and almost immediately coveted Enlightenment. (6H)

The Black Guardian   The White Guardian

BLACK HOLE OF TARTARUS
A space region near the flight path of the Hyperion III through which Bruchner tried to pilot the space ship. (7C)

BLACK LIGHT
Ultra-violet rays which, when passed through a converter, powered Drathro and his fellow robots from Andromeda. (7A)

THE BLACK ORCHID
Proving the existence of this South American flower became an obsession with George Cranleigh and he wrote a book on the subject. Later he ventured to that continent and discovered the flower in a jungle but was captured by the Kajabi tribe who cut out his tongue and drove him insane to protect their secret. (6A)

THE BLACK PYRAMID
The tomb in which Sutekh was imprisoned in Egypt. (4G)

BLACK SCORPION TONG
See TONG OF THE BLACK SCORPION

BLACK SCROLLS
The black scrolls contained forbidden knowledge concerning the Death Zone as recorded by Rassilon. When Borusa played the Game of Rassilon, he planted the black scrolls in the quarters of the current Castellan. Borusa hoped to throw suspicion of playing the Game of Rassilon on the Castellan. The black scrolls were finally inciner-

ated by a booby trap laid by the Lord President. (6K)

BLACKBEARD
The fictional villain summoned by the Master of the Land of Fiction to help in the battle against the Second Doctor's heroes. (UU)

BLADE, Captain
The pilot whose body print was exchanged for the second-in-command of the Chameleons. (KK)

BLAKE, Corporal
A member of Colonel Pemberton's patrol during the Yeti occupation of the London Underground. He choked to death, smothered by a blast from their web-guns. (QQ)

BLAKE, Josiah
The King's Revenue Officer who helped the First Doctor against the smugglers in Cornwall. (CC)

BLINOVITCH LIMITATION EFFECT
Time-reversing act named after the Russian scientist who turned himself back into a baby as referred to by the Third Doctor. (KKK, WWW, 6F)

BLOCK TRANSFER
The technique of manipulating the structure of the space-time continuum mastered by the

Logopolitans and employed by Adric to form a projection. (5V, 5Z)

BLOODAXE
The Lieutenant of Irongron's bunch of cut-throats. (UUU)

BLOR
Queen Thalira's champion who was destroyed by the heat ray of the fake Aggedor. (YYY)

BLUE FLAME
The product of gases forcing their way up a geological fault from the heart of a planet which exists on both Karn and Sarn; on the former the Elixir of Life is distilled from it. (4K, 6Q)

BLYTHE, 3rd Officer Jane
The naval officer who acted as secretary and personal assistant to Captain Hart at H.M.S. Seaspite. (LLL)

BOAZ
A member of a guerilla task force from the 22nd century who travelled back 200 years to execute Sir Reginald Styles in an attempt to change history so that the Daleks would not become rulers of the Earth in their time. He died fighting a Dalek. (KKK)

BOB
A technician and number 7 on the Moonbase in 2070. (HH)

BOK
A stone gargoyle in the cavern beneath the church in Devil's End. It was brought to life by the Master invoking the power of Azal and used by the renegade Time Lord in his scheme to obtain that power for himself. (JJJ)

BONDOT
The assassin hired to shoot Gaspard de Coligny. He failed because of Steven's warning and only wounded the Admiral. (W)

BOR
One of the Vanir enslaved on Terminus. (6G)

THE BORAD
The ruler of the planet Karfel. A mutant, half-Karfelon and half-Morlox, who came

Borad

into being when the Karfelon scientist Megelon was accidentally sprayed with Mustakozene 80 while experimenting on a Morlox. During a struggle with the Sixth Doctor he fell into his own Timelash. (6Y)

BORG
One of the crew of the sandminer on which the TARDIS materialised. He was killed by one of the Robots of Death. (4R)

BORGIA FAMILY
The notorious Italian family, as one of whom Captain Tancredi (one of the slivers of Scaroth) managed to pass himself off. (5H)

BORKAR
A Space Special Security agent. (V)

BORLASE, Thomas
An 18th century geologist who surveyed the Nine Travellers and then was crushed by one of the Ogri. (5C)

BORS
The bullying leader of the prisoners on Desperus, where he was eventually electrocuted. (V)

BORUSA
The Doctor's tutor at the Time Lord Academy on Gallifrey. Later he became interested in politics and eventually acceded to Cardinal of the Prydonian Chapter (4P). He rose to the rank of Chancellor (4Z) and when the Doctor left Gallifrey after thwarting the

Borusa (6E)

attempted invasion by the Vardans and the Sontarans, he was made acting President. He held this office through the crisis when Omega tried to cross into the positive universe (6E). It was during this period that he was impersonated by the White Guardian when he sent Romana to become the Doctor's companion (5A). During his time as President he became obsessed with a lust for power and yearned to be President Eternal and live forever. He foolishly invoked the use of the timescoop in order to play the Game of Rassilon and met his destiny at the whim of that first and greatest of the Time Lords when he was granted an eternity of living death in the Dark Tower. (6K)

BOSCOMBE MOOR
The land where the stone circle known as the Nine Travellers existed. (5C)

BOSSARD, Woris
The author of *Extinct Civilisations*, a book recalled by the Doctor which mentions the solar fireball which all but destroyed Ravolox. (7A)

BOSTOCK
The squire to Grandmaster Orcini. He was killed by the Daleks after he had shot Davros in the hand. (6Z)

BOTCHERBY, Oscar
An amateur lepidopterist and 'resting' actor temporarily employed as the manager of the La Cadenas restaurant in the Arab quarter of Seville. He was killed by Shockeye. (6W)

BOVEM
One of the members of the Dulcian Council at the time of the Doctor's second visit there. (TT)

BOWMAN,
Leading Telegraphist
One of Captain Hart's staff at H.M.S. Seaspite. (LLL)

BOZE, Trooper
A member of Chellak's squad on Androzani Minor. He was killed by the Magma Creature. (6R)

BRAGEN
The would-be ruler of the Vulcan colony in 2020. He allied himself with the Daleks but was shot by Valmar. (EE)

BRAK
A region of islands on the planet Thoros Beta from where the body into which Kiv's brain was transplanted was found adrift. (7B)

BRANWELL, Major
The commander of the Henlow Downs Missile Base. (VV)

BRAUN
A member of Sorenson's expedition to Zeta-Minor who was destroyed by the anti-matter creature. (4H)

BRAZEN
The Chief Orderly and Captain Revere's

second-in-command on Frontios. He was killed saving Turlough from the Tractators' excavating machine. (6N)

BRENDON SCHOOL
The school in Weston-super-Mare where the Brigadier taught mathematics after retiring from UNIT. For some time Turlough was a pupil at the school during his exile on Earth. (6F, 6Q)

BRENT
The deputy to Gia Kelly at T-mat control in the 22nd century. He was killed by oxygen starvation caused by one of the Ice Warriors' seed pods. (XX)

BRETT, Professor
The scientist who developed WOTAN and became 'possessed' by it and helped to organise the construction of *The War Machines*. (BB)

BREWSTER
The butler at Cranleigh Hall. (6A)

THE BRIGADIER
See LETHBRIDGE STEWART, Brigadier Alastair Gordon.

BRIGGS, Captain
The lady commander of the freighter sent back through time by the Cybermen. It was on her ship that Adric perished. (6B)

BRIGGS, Captain Benjamin
The Captain of the Marie Celeste, the crew

of which abandoned her when the Daleks landed aboard her. (R)

Briggs

BRIGGS, Samantha
A Liverpudlian girl who met the Second Doctor and Jamie when she came to Gatwick Airport to try to find out about her missing brother Brian. She helped them defeat the Chameleons. (KK)

BRIGHTON
The Sussex town where the Fourth Doctor attempted to take Leela (4V) and from where he and Romana set off for Argolis (5N) and on the sea front of which the Brigadier was given a watch by Doris. (ZZZ)

BRISBANE
The Australian city from which Tegan Jovanka and her cousin Colin Frazer originated. The Doctor mentions that Magnus Greel was known as 'The Butcher of Brisbane'. (4S, 5V, 5Z, 6E)

BRITTANICUS BASE
The scientific establishment in Britain during the Second Ice Age of 3000 commanded

by Clent. Its function was to monitor and check the advance of a glacier for which purpose it maintained a giant ioniser. (OO)

BROCK
The business adviser on Earth for the Argolin. He was impersonated in the Leisure Hive by a member of the West Lodge Foamasi. (5N)

BROKEN TOOTH
A former inhabitant of Marb Station on Ravolox who was ordered to be culled by Drathro. With the help of Merdeen he escaped and became a member of the Tribe of the Free, but was subsequently killed by the L-3 robot. (7A)

BROMLEY, John
A power technician at Operation Inferno who, infected by the green slime from the output pipe, degenerated into a Primord. (DDD)

BRONTOSAURUS
One of the dinosaurs transported to London by Professor Whitaker's timescoop (WWW). It was also mentioned by the Doctor minutes after his third regeneration. (4A)

BROOK, Congressman
The leader of the opposition on Earth in 2540. (QQQ)

BROOK COTTAGE
The residence of Sam and Meg Seeley and their dog, Darkie, near Ashbridge. (AAA)

BROOKES
One of Lieutenant Scott's troopers who fought against the Cybermen on Captain Briggs' freighter. (6B)

BROTADAC, Lieutenant
A Gaztak and second-in-command to Grugger. He was killed when the planet Zolfa-Thura blew up. (5Q)

BROTON
The Zygon warlord who impersonated the Duke of Forgill. He was killed by the Brigadier. (4F)

BROWNROSE
The bureaucratic civil servant of whom the Third Doctor got the better during the Nestenes' second attempted invasion of Earth. (EEE)

BRUCE, Donald
The Security Commissioner at the Kanowa Research Centre. (PP)

BRUCHNER
One of the assistants of Sarah Lasky who was killed by the Vervoids. (7C)

BRUMMEL, Beau
The Georgian lord with an extravagant style of dress, whom the Doctor mentions he has met. (G)

BRUNNER
A councillor on the planet Karfel. He fell into the Timelash in a struggle with Mykros. (6Y)

BRUS
A planet visited by Tryst's expedition. (5K)

BRYSON, Corporal
A UNIT soldier whose clumsy entry into its emergency HQ permitted the Third Doctor and Sergeant Benton to overcome the irrational Captain Yates during 'Operation Golden Age'. (WWW)

THE BUCCANEER
The name of the Beta Dart spaceship piloted by Dervish. (YY)

THE BUCCANEER
The ship captained by Wrack used in the Eternals' race for Enlightenment. (6H)

'The Buccaneer', Beta Dart

BUCKINGHAM, Lady Jennifer
One of the participants in the *War Games* in the World War I zone. She was deconditioned by the Second Doctor and helped him towards the defeat of the War Lord. (ZZ)

BULIC
One of the personnel of Sea-Base Four and one of the few survivors of the assault on it by the Silurians and Sea-Devils. (6L)

BULLER FAMILY
Housewife Emma Buller was abducted and had her life-force drained from her by Magnus Greel. When her husband Joseph, a cabdriver, tackled Li H'sen Chang about her disappearance he was murdered by members of the Tong of the Black Scorpion on Chang's orders. (4S)

THE BUNKER
The scientific research headquarters, located four miles from the Kaled dome, where Davros created the Daleks. (4E)

BURNS
The r/t operator at Snowcap base in 1986. (DD)

BURNS, Sergeant-Major
One of the conditioned British participants in the *War Games* in the World War I zone. (ZZ)

THE BUTCHER OF BRISBANE
The infamous nickname attributed to the 51st century war criminal, Magnus Greel. (4S)

BUTLER
A conspirator in 'Operation Golden Age' who served both as Whitaker's assistant and Grover's chauffeur. (WWW)

Cargo Ship C-982

C.19
The department from which the civil servant Sir John Sudbury, the head of UNIT in Britain, worked. (6C)

C-982
The Earth cargo ship plundered by Ogrons (using the Master's hypno-sound device to appear as Draconians) and on which the TARDIS subsequently materialised in 2540. (QQQ)

C531
The virus strain with which the Fourth Doctor was able to overcome the Nucleus of the Swarm and its breeding tanks on Titan. (4T)

C E T Machine
The Continuous Event Transmitter Machine. It was invented by Professor Stein and developed by his colleague Doctor Tryst

and constituted a crude form of matter transfer by dimensional control. (5K)

C I A
The Celestial Intervention Agency. Although the basis of Time Lord philosophy precludes interference in the affairs of the Universe, from time to time such interference becomes urgent and necessary. Such operations are under the control of the ultra-secret CIA which is composed of Time Lords of the highest rank. (4P)

C V E
Charged Vacuum Emboitment. A whirlpool-like void between universes, several of which were created by the Logopolitans in order to dispose of entropy (5V). It was through one of these that the Great Vampire (5P), the Hydrax (5P) and Rorvik's ship (5S) entered E-space as well as how the TARDIS was drawn there (5R) and left it. (5S)

THE CABER
The ghillie to the Duke of Forgill, impersonated by the Zygons. (4F)

THE CAILLEACH
The goddess of War, Death and Magic worshipped by members of the British Institute of Druidic Studies. (5C)

CALDER, Sergeant
The army sergeant who was part of the squad assigned to guard the Movellan nerve

gas cylinders. He was killed on the orders of the Daleks and duplicated. (6P)

CALDWELL
The Chief Mineralogist of the IMC squad on Uxarius in 2972. He helped the Third Doctor, Jo and the colonists against his commander Captain Dent and the Master (HHH).

CALIB
A member of the tribe of the Sevateem who seized control of it once its leader, Andor, was killed. (4Q)

CALLUM, Jim
The First Officer of the Space Orbiter which took the archaeological party to Telos in the 25th century. He was wounded by a shot from a cyber-gun fired by Eric Kleig. (MM)

CALUFRAX
A planet, in reality the second segment of the Key to Time, robbed of its mineral wealth and energy, shrunk and kept in his trophy room by the Captain. (5B)

CAMARA, Senhora
One of the past identities adopted by Cessair of Diplos. (5C)

CAMBRIDGE
The city in which Liz Shaw researched science at the University (AAA) and returned to stay; where the Master built TOMTIT at the Newton Institute in the

suburb of Wootton (OOO); and where the Fourth Doctor was visiting when the Timescoop attempted to transport him to Gallifrey (6K).

CAMECA
An elderly Aztec woman who helped the time travellers when they were trapped in Central America in the 15th century. She became very fond of the First Doctor and went through an engagement ceremony with him! (F)

Cameca

CAMFORD, Victor
The governor of Stangmoor prison. (FFF)

CAMILLA
The name adopted by Navigation Officer Lauren Macmillan of the Earth spaceship

Hydrax, when she became Queen and one of the Three Who Rule on the planet in E-space where the Hydrax was drawn by the Great Vampire. She and her vampiric companions, Zargo and Aukon, crumbled to dust when the Fourth Doctor successfully destroyed the Great Vampire. (5P)

CAMPBELL

A member of UNIT staff working in the Scientific Supplies Section. He was telephoned by Jo for supplies for the Third Doctor's use during the second attempted invasion of Earth by the Nestenes. (EEE)

CAMPBELL, David

A member of Dortmun's resistance fighters in 2164. Susan fell in love with him and stayed in 22nd century Earth to marry him. (K)

CAPABLANCA

The Russian chess-master whom the Doctor mentions he has met. (5D)

CAPEL, Taren

A mad scientist raised by robots. He tried to create a robot rebellion on a sandminer, having substituted himself for Dask, one of its crew-members, but failed when his neck was broken by SV.7. (4R)

THE CAPITOL

The city on Gallifrey which is the centre of the Time Lord society. (4P, 4Z, 6D, 6K, 7C)

THE CAPTAIN

A cyborg rebuilt by Queen Xanxia when he crash-landed on her planet of Zanak. His technological knowledge adapted the planet so that it could travel through space and materialise around others to rob them of their mineral wealth and also their energy which was needed to sustain Xanxia's time dams. He ruled the planet as a sort of regent until Xanxia's projection killed him when he rebelled against her, following her disinterested and compassionless stance after the death of his friend, Fibuli. (5B)

CARDINAL

The leader of one of the Time Lord Chapters on Gallifrey.

CARIS

A Savant, one of the scientific and technical caste on the planet Tigella. (5Q)

CARNEY, Mick

The engineer in charge of gas drilling Rig D in the North Sea in the 1970s. He was taken over by the Weed. (RR)

THE CAROLLERS

A pop music group popular in the 1960s; later known as The Commonmen. (A)

CARRINGTON, General

The commanding officer of the Space Security Department and former astronaut on Recovery 6. He was a man obsessed with keeping the Earth free from alien contamination and staged an elaborate hoax to incriminate the ambassadors he met on Mars. (CCC)

The Carsenome

THE CARSENOME
The centre from which the Animus controlled the Zarbi. (N)

CARSON
One of the crew on the freighter commanded by Captain Briggs. He was killed by the Cybermen. (6B)

CARSTAIRS, Lieutenant Jeremy
One of the participants in the *War Games* in the World War I zone. He was deconditioned by the Second Doctor and helped him in the defeat of the War Lord. (ZZ)

Lieutenant Carstairs

CARTER
One of the Expeditionary Team sent to Deva-Loka under the command of Sanders. He had disappeared before the TARDIS materialised there. (5Y)

CARTER
One of Lieutenant Scott's troopers. He was killed by the Cybermen's androids. (6B)

CARTER, Doctor
A member of staff in the pathology lab at Nunton Hospital. He died, falling from a catwalk, when he attacked the Fourth Doctor, having been taken over by the will of Eldrad. (4N)

CASALI, Enrico
The Italian r/t operator on the *Wheel in Space*. (SS)

CASEY
The Irish doorman and caretaker of the Palace Theatre. He was killed by Magnus Greel. (4S)

CASS
A member of one of the founding families on the world where the Fourth Doctor encountered the *Robots of Death*. He was strangled by a robot aboard the sandminer where he was a crew-member. (4R)

CASS, Ensign
A member of Chellak's squad on Androzani Minor. Apart from Chellak and the Salateen

android, only he was aware of how Sharaz Jek saved the Fifth Doctor and Peri from death under the Red Hood. To save face Chellak sent him on a suicide mission. (6R)

CASSANDRA
The Trojan prophetess to whom Katarina was hand-maiden and who was doomed to be able to predict the future accurately, but to have no one believe her. She was the daughter of Priam and the sister of Paris. She was slaughtered in the Greek assault. (U)

CASSIDY, Miss
The matron at Brendon School. (6F)

CASSIOPEIA
The constellation where the Fourth Doctor attempted to take Sarah-Jane for a holiday (4L) and with which the Master aligned a C V E from the Pharos Project. (5V)

CASSIUS
A planet in the solar system further away than Pluto, mentioned by the Doctor. (4W)

CASTELLAN
The Commander of the Chancellery Guard on Gallifrey who is responsible for all security in the Capitol.

CASTLE, Nigel
A novelist and the real name of Adam, whom Sarah-Jane encountered on the 'spaceship' at the time of 'Operation Golden Age'. (WWW)

CATHAY
The city in China to which Marco Polo forced the First Doctor to travel in the hope that he would receive his freedom in return for his gift to Kublai Khan – the TARDIS. It was also known as Shang-Tu. (D)

CATS
Feline Earth animals for which the Sixth Doctor had a predilection, often wearing a brooch depicting one on his lapel.

CAVE OF 500 EYES
A cave at Tun-Huang, which by legend was one of the hideouts of the followers of Ala-eddin. Barbara explored it and was held prisoner there by Malik. (D)

CAVEN, Maurice
The leader of the space pirates on Lobos. He was killed when his spaceship exploded under attack by Warne. (YY)

CELATION
One of the delegates allied with the Daleks when they attempted to carry out their Master Plan. (V)

THE CELEBRATION CHIMES
A joyful sound played in the Panopticon on the election of a president of Gallifrey. They were sounded at 50 times the volume by Borusa to enable the Fourth Doctor to escape from the Sontarans. (4Z)

CELERY
A green vegetable which turns purple in the presence of gases in the Praxis range to which the Doctor is allergic. He wore a stalk of it on his lapel in his fifth incarnation.

CELESTIAL TOYMAKER
The enigmatic seeming-magician who diverted the TARDIS in flight to his domain, rendered the First Doctor intangible and

Clara The Clown And
The Celestial Toymaker

dumb and forced him to play the Trilogic Game while Steven and Dodo were set a series of tasks to win back the time machine. He and the Doctor had had a fleeting former acquaintance but on their second meeting the villain was set to achieve maximum amusement from their time together. He was defeated by the Doctor's abilities of mimicry and ventriloquism and his realm vanished. (Y)

CENTRAL REGISTER

The nub of the computer system on Logopolis and a logical copy of the Pharos Project on Earth. (5V)

CEREBRATON MENTOR

The emotion inducing device developed by Professor Watkins and used against the Cybermen. (VV)

CERENKOV

A scientist in the field of radiation after whom Cerenkov radiation wave equations are named, mentioned by Romana. (5N)

CESSAIR

A criminal from the planet Diplos guilty of murder and the removal and misuse of the Great Seal of Diplos. She hid out on Earth for nearly four thousand years and masqueraded as the Cailleach and other identities including Lady Montcalm, Mrs Trefusis, Senhora Camara, the Mother Superior of the Convent of the Little Sisters of St Gudula and Vivien Fay. (5C)

CETES
A constellation between which and Sculptor (another constellation) the TARDIS materialised in a temporal void. (6V)

CHACAWS
A fiercely-spiked fruit grown in the penal plantations of Androzani Major. (6R)

CHAL
The leader of *The Savages*. (AA)

CHALMERS, Sergeant
A UNIT soldier on duty at the raid on Devil's End to prevent the Master from succeeding in obtaining Azal's power for himself. (JJJ)

CHAMBERS, J J
The pseudonymous owner of the Fantasy Factory in the Victorian England setting in the Matrix, in reality the Valeyard. (7C)

CHAMBERS, Joseph
The junior Cabinet Minister, responsible for security, killed by Jeremiah Kettlewell's Robot on the orders of Hilda Winters. (4A)

CHAMELEONS
An alien race which had suffered a catastrophe when one of their nuclear reactors exploded leaving the whole population of their planet faceless and sterile. They attempted to replace Earth people by kidnapping them and substituting members of

Chameleon Tours

their own race using the front of a holiday tours firm based at Gatwick Airport until the Second Doctor foiled their plans and gave them some ideas for a solution to their identity crisis. (KK)

CHAMPION, Corporal
The UNIT soldier assigned to guard Collinson. (CCC)

CHANCELLERY GUARDS
The security forces in the Capitol on Gallifrey which report to the Castellan.

CHANCELLOR
The second in authority to the President of the High Council on Gallifrey.

CHANDLER, Will
The youth from 1643 transported to Little Hodcome in 1984 by a time-confusion caused by the Malus. (6M)

CHANDLING, Lady
A neighbour of Harrison Chase. (4L)

CHANG, Ken
A Chinese member of the crew of the *Wheel in Space*. He was killed by the Cybermen. (SS)

CHANNING
An Earthman who was disposed of by the Nestenes and replaced by an Auton replica which assumed control of George Hibbert's plastics factory in order to spearhead the planned invasion of Earth by the octopoid-like intelligences. (AAA)

CHAPAL
The deceased father of Ixta, the Aztec commander. He designed and built the tomb of Yetaxa, and the Garden of Peace in which the retired of the Aztec tribe spent their days. (F)

CHAPLETTE, Anne
A serving girl on the staff of the Abbot of Amboise. She was born and raised in Vassy where her Protestant father had been killed in a Huguenot massacre by the Catholics. She became involved in the plot to assassinate Admiral de Coligny and was hidden in his household by Steven under the alias of Genevieve. It is possible that she was an ancestor of Dodo. (W)

Anne Chaplette

CHARGE OF THE LIGHT BRIGADE
The incident during the Crimean War which the Doctor mentions he has witnessed. (LL, LLL)

CHARGED VACUUM EMBOITMENT
See C V E.

CHARLES
The son of the squire in 17th century England whose manor house was taken over

by the Terileptils. He was killed by them. (5X)

CHARLES IX
The King of France at the time of the Saint Bartholomew's Eve Massacre. (W)

CHARLIE
The barman of the Last Chance Saloon in Tombstone. He was shot by Johnny Ringo. (Z)

CHARLIE
The eighth member of the crew of the Moonbase. (HH)

CHARLIE
One of the inmates of Stangmoor Prison involved in the attempted prison breakout. (FFF)

CHARLIE
The nickname given to the Mk III servo-robot used by Morgan of IMC to give the impression of attacks by giant lizards on the Earth colonists on Uxarius. (HHH)

CHARLIE
One of the BBC-3 crew technicians involved in covering Professor Horner's opening of the Devil's Hump barrow outside Devil's End at Beltane. (JJJ)

CHARLIE
The postmaster of the village of Devil's End. (JJJ)

CHARO CHARO EGAN
The call sign of the Space Security Service headquarters on Earth in 4000. (V)

CHASE, Harrison
The millionaire botanist who coveted the Krynoid seed pods and was crushed to death in his own compost machine. (4L)

CHEDAKI, Marshal
The military commander of the Kraal invasion force. (4J)

CHELA
An assistant to Ambril on Manussa. (6D)

CHELLAK, General
The leader of the military squad on Androzani Minor. He died caught in a mud burst there. (6R)

CHELSEA
The part of London turned into a heliport by the Daleks (K) and the location of the antique shop used by Edward Waterfield to which he was ordered by the Daleks to bring the Second Doctor and Jamie. (LL)

CHEN, Mavic
The Guardian of the Solar System in 4000 who traitorously allied himself with the Daleks and helped them when the First Doctor attempted to frustrate their Master Plan. He was finally killed by them. (V)

Mavic Chen

CHENCHU
The manager of the way-station at Lop. (D)

CHENG TEIK, General
The leader of the Chinese delegation to the World Peace Conference who was murdered, on the Master's instruction, by Captain Chin Lee. (FFF)

CHENG-TUNG
A way-station visited by the First Doctor in the company of Marco Polo, on the journey to Cathay. It was also known as the White City. (D)

CHERUB
The pirate who double-crossed his captain, Samuel Pike, and was consequently killed by him. (CC)

CHESSENE O'THE FRANZINE GRIG
Dastari's chatelaine, an Androgum which he had technologically augmented to mega-genius level. She was destroyed by molecular disintegration in the Kartz-Reimer time module. (6W)

CHESTER, Doctor
The leader of the party from South Bend Base who rescued the Fourth Doctor and Sarah-Jane in Antarctica. (4L)

CHIN LEE, Captain
A member of the Chinese delegation to the World Peace Conference. Under the influence of the Master she wrought havoc and committed murder until the Third Doctor removed his telepathic amplifier from her and freed her. (FFF)

CHINN, Horatio
A pompous bureaucrat from the Ministry of Defence who crossed swords with the Third Doctor during the encounter with Axos. (GGG)

Chessene O'The Franzine Grig

CHLORIS
An extremely fertile planet where metal was in very short supply. (5G)

CHO-JE
A Tibetan monk at the meditation centre in Mummerset who was in actuality a projection of the future body of the Time Lord K'anpo. (ZZZ)

CHORLEY, Harold
The television reporter and interviewer assigned to cover the Yeti occupation of the London Underground for the media. (QQ)

THE CHOSEN
Those of the Earth's population preserved in the cryogenic chambers on Space Station Nerva. (4C)

CHOSEN ONE
The ruler of the Sarns who traditionally was born in fire. Malkon had been proclaimed a Chosen One because he was found as a baby in the flaming wreckage of the ship on which his father was exiled from Trion. Turlough was able to claim the right to be a Chosen One when Malkon was shot down by an elder by virtue that the brothers were both branded with the Misos Triangle. (6Q)

CHRONIC HYSTERESIS
A fold in time and another term for a time-loop. (5Q)

CHRONODYNE
The crystalline material from which the Fourth Doctor moulded the imitation Sixth Segment of the Key to Time. (5F)

CHUB
A government mineralogist and crew-member of the sandminer on which the TARDIS materialised. He was strangled by one of the Robots of Death. (4R)

CHUMBLIES
The name with which Vicki dubbed the robots belonging to the Rills. (T)

CHUN-SEN
A scientist of the future who dabbled in the science of time travel, mentioned by the Third Doctor. (WWW)

CIVIC TRANSPORT MUSEUM
The museum from which Barbara and Jenny 'borrowed' a dustcart to flee the Daleks in London and make their way to Bedfordshire. (K)

CLANCEY, Milo
A miner and former partner of Dom Issigri in mining Argonite on Ta, who was a 'legend' in his youth on Rega Magnum because of his eccentricity. (YY)

CLANGERS
A BBC television programme watched by

the Master during his confinement following his trial for his dealings at Devil's End. (LLL)

CLANTON FAMILY
The Clanton brothers Ike, Phineas and Billy, spurred on by their Pa, sought revenge on Doc Holliday for having shot another brother, Reuben. The First Doctor became embroiled in the situation between Holliday and the Earp brothers which culminated in the Gunfight at the OK Corral outside Tombstone, Arizona in 1881. (Z)

CLARA THE CLOWN
One of the opponents for Steven and Dodo in their enforced game of Blind Man's Buff in the realm of the Celestial Toymaker. (Y)

CLARK, Alan
One of the crew of the oil rig which was one of the first targets of the Sea Devils. (LLL)

CLEGG, Professor Hubert
A fake mind-reader who actually possessed the power of psychokinesis. He was killed when he handled the crystal from Metebelis Three during an ESP experiment conducted by the Third Doctor. (ZZZ)

CLEMENTS, Ernie
The poacher who became trapped behind the deflection barrier surrounding Marcus Scarman's house and was crushed to death between two Servicers. (4G)

CLENT
The commander of Brittanicus base in 3000. (OO)

CLEOPATRA
The celebrated queen of Egypt whom the Doctor implies that he has met. (4M)

CLIFFORD, Angela
A stewardess on Concorde Golf Victor Foxtrot. (6C)

CLOCKWORK SOLDIERS
The menacing guards in the Land of Fiction. (WW)

CLONE
A replication of an individual using a single cell of that individual as a focus. Clones retain the character of the original organism.

The Drahvins (T) and the Sontarans (UUU, 4B, 4Z, 6W) are cloned races and the Borad employed a clone of himself to distract the Sixth Doctor (6Y). The Doctor has been cloned himself in his fourth incarnation, using the Kilbracken technique, as was Leela. (4T)

Clockwork Soldier

CLOVEN HOOF
The public house in the village of Devil's End of which the landlord, Bert Walker, was mesmerised by the Master into trying to kill the Third Doctor. (JJJ)

CLOWNS
The opponents for Steven and Dodo in their

enforced game of Blind Man's Buff in the realm of the Celestial Toymaker. (Y)

COAL HILL SCHOOL
The school where Ian Chesterton taught chemistry and Barbara Wright taught history to their pupils including one registered at the school as Susan Foreman. (A)

COALMEN, THE
A pop group – full name John Smith and the Coalmen – whose latest record Susan heard on her transistor radio. (A)

COCKERILL, Corporal
One of the orderlies on Frontios. When an action of the Fifth Doctor caused the malfunction of the Tractators' traction device, it appeared that he saved himself from being sucked into the ground. The less-fortunate of Frontios hailed him as a leader for their rebellion upon witnessing the event. (6N)

COCKTAIL POLLY
A mixture of the solvents acetone, benzene, ether, epoxy and propane with which Ben, Polly and Jamie attacked the Cybermen on the Moonbase in 2070. (HH)

CODAL
A member of the Thal suicide squad which defeated the Daleks on Spiridon. (SSS)

COLBERT, Léon
A friend of Jules Renan, who flirted with Barbara. Actually he was loyal to the revolu-

Codal

tion and captured Ian in order to elicit information about James Stirling. He was shot by Renan. (H)

COLBERT, Roger
The temporary secretary to the Abbot of Amboise. (W)

COLBY, Professor Adam
The assistant to Dr Fendleman and the person who discovered the 12 million year old skull. (4X)

COLIN
One of the people whom Salamander had tricked into believing that the world of 2017 was contaminated and so they stayed in an underground nuclear shelter for five years and unknowingly helped his scheme by engineering 'natural' disasters. (PP)

THE COLLECTOR
An Usurian and the managing director of The Company. Unable to deal with the inflation the Fourth Doctor had introduced into its computer, the collector shrank to its original form and was bottled by him. (4W)

COLLIER
One of the crew of the Edwardian sailing-ship utilised by Striker in his race with his fellow Eternals. (6H)

COLLINS
The butler to Marcus Scarman who was strangled by a Servicer. (4G)

COLLINS, Private
A UNIT soldier and part of the squad on duty when the Third Doctor was menaced by a dinosaur thanks to Captain Yates having sabotaged the doctor's stun-gun. (WWW)

COLLINSON
The rogue sergeant in the Space Security Department captured by the Brigadier when UNIT tracked the transmission of a reply message to Recovery 7 to a warehouse. (CCC)

COLVILLE, Crewmaster
One of the crew of Nerva Beacon killed by the 'plague' of cybermats. He had a brother who was the First Officer on the Pluto–Earth flight diverted from the Beacon. (4C)

COMPANION OF THE KROTONS
The dubious honour conferred on Gonds with good intelligence. In fact once aboard the Dynatrope their brains were drained of their energy by the Krotons. (WW)

THE COMPANY
The entity which constructed the artificial suns around Pluto. (4W)

CONDO
A slow-witted convict who crash-landed on Karn in a Dravidian spaceship. He was rescued by Mehendri Solon who replaced his

injured arm with a hook by micro neurosurgery and to whom he became servant. He died saving Sarah-Jane from the Morbius-monster. (4K)

CONRAD OF TYRE
The ruler with whom Saladin wished to make a treaty and to whom he sent the merchant Luigi Ferrigo as his emissary. (P)

CONSCIENCE OF MARINUS
A vast computer and the ultimate deterrent for war on the planet of Marinus, watched over by Arbitan, its keeper, and destroyed after a fake component was inserted by the Voord leader, Yartek. (E)

The Conscience Of Marinus

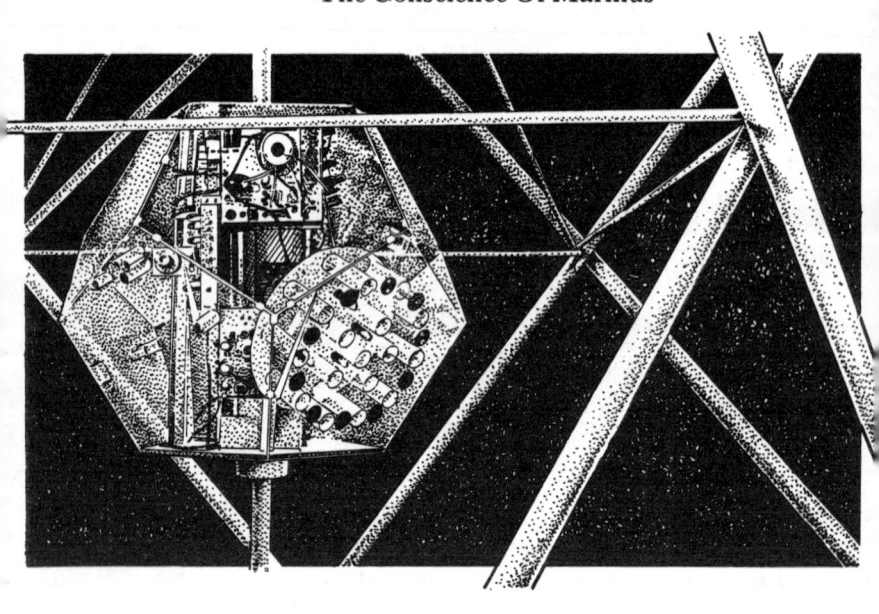

CONSULS
The rulers of the Traken Union of which there were five in number. (5T)

CONSUM BANK
The bank on Pluto which the Fourth Doctor attempted to defraud to save Leela from Mandrel's rebels. (4W)

THE CONTROLLER
The leader of an Earth colony in the future who was in fact a puppet behind whom the Macra ruled and eventually killed. (JJ)

The Controller (KKK)

THE CONTROLLER
Though considered to be a senior Government official on 22nd century Earth under Dalek rule, the Controller was in fact a superior slave whose superiority stemmed from receiving a few privileges in return for helping to oppress his fellow humans. In return for the Third Doctor sparing his life he helped him and Jo to escape the Daleks, for which 'crime' they exterminated him. (KKK)

CONVENT OF THE LITTLE SISTERS OF SAINT GUDULA
The religious house built on the same site as the home of Leonard de Vries. (5C)

COOK, Doctor Humphrey
A civil servant, chairman of the Grants Committee and friend of Doctor Perceval, the director of the Newton Institute at Wootton where he attended a demonstration of TOMTIT. (OOO)

COOLIE
A member of the Tong of the Black Scorpion who helped to murder Joseph Buller. He committed suicide on the orders of Li H'sen Chang. (4S)

COORDINATOR
The head of the Records Section in the Capitol on Gallifrey. (4P)

CORDO
The D grade factory worker for The Company on Pluto. Saved from committing suicide by the Fourth Doctor because of his inability to pay the unjust taxes levied by The Company, he was inspired to lead a successful revolt against his employers. (4W)

CORELLIS
An Alzarian scientist who existed fifty years before the Fourth Doctor's visit there. (5R)

CORNISH, Professor Ralph
The Director of Space Control Centre. (CCC)

THE CORONET OF RASSILON
The Coronet of Rassilon permitted its wearer to control the minds of others. Borusa used it against the Fifth Doctor whilst playing the Game of Rassilon. (6K)

CORONIC ACID
A liquid deadly to the cloned tissue of Sontarans, a squadron of whom was decimated by the Rutans at Volotha with shells filled with it. Copying this tactic, Chessene used it to destroy Stike and Varl. (6W)

CORWYN, Doctor Gemma
The widowed Medical Officer and second-in-command of the *Wheel in Space*. She was killed by a Cyberman. (SS)

CORY, Marc

An agent of the Space Security Service who on his own initiative investigated reported mysterious happenings on the planet Kembel. He was killed by the Daleks. (T/A)

Marc Cory

COSMIC SCIENCE

Both the Doctor and the Master hold degrees in this subject from the Time Lord Academy but the latter's is of a higher grade than the former's. (EEE)

COSTA, Landing Officer

One of the excise officials sent from Azure to investigate the space accident involving the Empress and the Hecate. (5K)

COSWORTH, Major

A member of UNIT who helped the Brigadier plan the assault on Stangmoor Prison. (FFF)

COTTON

A Skybase security guard who rebelled against the tyrannical Marshal and helped the Third Doctor and Jo to overthrow him and restore the rule of the planet Solos to its own people. (NNN)

COVENT GARDEN
The area of London where the War Machines were constructed (BB) and in the London Underground station of which the TARDIS materialised in the 1970s. (QQ)

CRAB NEBULA
A cloud of cosmic waste matter which had been a sun until the superbeings on Uxarius tested their doomsday weapon, as described by the Master. (HHH)

CRADDOCK, Jack
A prisoner on the Dalek saucer, Alpha Major. (K)

CRANE, Lieutenant
One of the conditioned British participants in the *War Games* in the World War I zone. (ZZ)

CRANLEIGH FAMILY
The family who resided at Cranleigh Hall where the Fifth Doctor was wrongfully arrested for the murder of the footman, James. The elder son, George, discovered the Black Orchid in South America for which the Kajabi Indians cut out his tongue and drove him insane. In this state he killed two servants, Digby and James, and menaced Nyssa, who was a double of his fiancée, Ann Talbot. He fell to his death from the roof of Cranleigh Hall. He was succeeded by his cricketing brother, Charles, as Marquis of Cranleigh. Their doting mother, Margaret, tried to cover up George's acts of violence in conspiracy with his friend Dittar Latoni.

The house dominated the village of Cranleigh at the railway station of which, Cranleigh Halt, the TARDIS materialised in 1925. (6A)

CRATER OF NEEDLES
A part of Vortis where Menoptera were kept prisoner by Zarbi under the influence of the Animus. (N)

CRAWFORD, Doctor
A doctor at Wenley Hospital. (BBB)

CRAYFORD, Guy
A senior defence astronaut whom Styggron deceived into betraying Earth and subsequently shot. (4J)

'CREAG AN TUIRE'
The rally cry of the Clan McLaren, often uttered by Jamie.

CRESSIDA
The name adopted by Vicki when she visited Troy and elected to stay in that time period to marry Troilus. (U)

CRICHTON, Colonel Charles
The Brigadier's successor as head of the British UNIT forces, encountered by the Second Doctor. (6K)

CRICHTON, John
An athlete, and the real name of Mark whom Sarah-Jane encountered on the 'spaceship'

John Crichton (Mark)

at the time of 'Operation Golden Age'. (WWW)

CRICKET
The Earth sport for which the Fifth Doctor had a particular predilection. He often used a cricketing manoeuvre to extract him from a dilemma. (5W, 5Z, 6A, 6C, 6N)

CRINOTH
The planet from which the Nimon planned to travel to Skonnos. It was destroyed by a chain reaction of the Nimons' own making. (5L)

CRITAS
An Eternal who took part in the race for Enlightenment in a Greek vessel, which was sabotaged by Wrack. (6H)

CRITO
A council elder in Atlantis at the time of the Third Doctor's and Jo's visit there. (OOO)

CROSS
A trustee in the penal colony on the Moon in 2540. He pretended to help the Third Doctor and Professor Dale to escape from the prison but trapped them in an airlock. (QQQ)

CROSSLAND, Detective Inspector
The Scotland Yard detective sent to Gatwick Airport to investigate the disappearance of his colleague Detective Inspector Gascoigne.

He was captured by the Chameleons and substituted by their Director. (KK)

CROZIER
An alien scientist brought to Thoros Beta to operate on Kiv. (7B)

CRUICKSHANK, Doctor
A medic at the Bi-Al Foundation whose will was taken over by the Nucleus of the Swarm. He was shot down by K-9. (4T)

CRYONS
The indigenous population of Telos who live in sub-zero temperatures. They were almost wiped out by the Cybermen. (6T)

Cryon

CRYSTAL OF KRONOS
A crystal from Atlantis with which the Master sought to control Kronos the Chronivore. (OOO)

CULLINGFORTH, Lady
A parliamentarian, and the real name of Ruth whom Sarah-Jane encountered on the 'spaceship' at the time of 'Operation Golden Age'. (WWW)

CULLODEN
The battle of 1745 in which Jamie and the McLarens had taken part just prior to meeting the Second Doctor. (FF)

CULLY
The son of the Director of the Council of Dulkis. He helped the Second Doctor to defeat *The Dominators*. (TT)

CULSHAW, Dave
A steward on Concorde Golf Victor Foxtrot. (6C)

CULT OF MORBIUS
The name given to the band of people who followed the renegade ex-leader of the High Council of the Time Lords, of which Mehendri Solon was one. (4K)

CUMMINGS, Police Constable
One of the police officers called in to arrest the Fifth Doctor for the murder of James, the footman to the Cranleigh family. (6A)

CURLY
One of the crew of the hovercraft which twice attacked the Second Doctor believing him to be Salamander. He was killed in a helicopter explosion over the grounds of Astrid Ferrier's house. (PP)

CURT
The assistant to Peri's step-father, Howard Foster. (6Q)

THE CUSTODIANS
The victorious faction in the civil war on Trion which exiled the family of Turlough to Earth and Sarn. (6Q)

CUTLER, General
The commander of the Snowcap base in the Antarctic in 1986. He tried to unleash the

General Cutler And Krang

Z-bomb on Mondas to rescue his Lieutenant-astronaut son Terry from the Cybermen. He was killed by them. (DD)

CYBER CONTROLLER

The commander and motivator of cyber operations on Telos. He was badly damaged by the efforts of the Second Doctor, Jamie and Toberman in 2450 (MM) but was eventually repaired. He was finally destroyed by the Sixth Doctor and Lytton before the cyber base blew up. (6T)

CYBER-BOMBS

The devices strapped to the Fourth Doctor, Lester and Stevenson before they were transmitted to Voga (4D). The Fifth Doctor also defused one in the underground caves in which the TARDIS materialised in 2526 (6B) whilst Adric died in an anti-matter explosion sparked off by one. (6B)

A cyber-megatron bomb was the ultimate weapon which the Cybermen intended to use against Earth in 1975. It was destroyed by a Russian missile. (VV)

CYBERMATS

Cybernised rodents. They have the in-built ability to home in on brain waves, and are susceptible to gold dust. (MM, SS, 4D)

CYBERMEN

The Cybermen are beings who were once humanoid in form but who increased their strength and life-span by replacing their flesh and blood organs with metal and plastic. This had the effect of leaving them emotionless, and they retain none of their humanoid feelings and passions.

They originated from the tenth planet of Earth's solar system, Mondas (DD), which later wandered out of its orbit. They migrated to Telos, where they all but wiped out the indigenous population, the Cryons (6T). They never cease experimenting upon themselves and constantly seek to improve their outward 'armour'. Packs on their chests replaced their hearts and they possess built-in weaponry, which has been located in their helmets (4D) and also in their chest units (VV) as well as carrying hand weapons

Cybermen On The Moon Surface

(6B). Inside their helmets is an in-built distress signal which sounds should they become de-activated (6T). They usually divide into platoons led by a Cyber-leader and are motivated by a Cyber Controller on Telos. They are susceptible to gold dust (4D), high gravity (HH) and high radiation. (DD)

The First Doctor foiled their attempt to take over the Snowcap Space Tracking Station at the South Pole in 1986, an assault which ended in the destruction of Mondas. (DD) The Second Doctor frustrated their efforts on four occasions: on the lunar surface (HH), on Telos (MM), on the space station known as The Wheel (SS) and on Earth (VV) with the help of the newly-formed UNIT.

With the aid of the Vogans the Fourth Doctor prevented an assault on their planet by a squad which had invaded another space station (4D) and the Fifth Doctor stopped their renewed efforts against Earth, though at the expense of Adric's life (6B). Four of the first five of the Doctor's incarnations were hindered by several cyber patrols in the Death Zone on Gallifrey when forced to play the Game of Rassilon (6K) and the Sixth Doctor averted their attempt to change history and prevent the destruction of Mondas. (6T)

CYCLOPS
Odysseus' mute spy who was killed by the Trojans. (U)

CYCLOTRON
The reactor for converting energy to power at the Atomic Research Centre on Wenley

Moor which was siphoned by the Silurians. (BBB)

CYRIL
The mischievous but deadly schoolboy against whom Steven and Dodo were forced to play hopscotch in the realm of the Celestial Toymaker. (Y)

CYRRHENIS MINIMA
The planet which Garron and Unstoffe were on when the Fourth Doctor initially attempted to locate the first segment of the Key to Time. (5A)

CYTRONIC PARTICLE ACCELERATOR
A machine devised by Sutekh to power the Servicers. (4G)

D

D.84

D.84
A robotic agent of the company on whose sandminer the TARDIS materialised. It was destroyed trying to save the Fourth Doctor from the mad scientist Taren Capel. (4R)

DE_3O_2
The chemical formula of the contents of the jar in which Darrius hid the micro-circuit key to the 'Conscience of Marinus' entrusted to him by Arbitan. (E)

THE D J
The D J was an employee on the planet Necros, although alien to it. His function was to keep the comatose aware of current affairs while also keeping their brains amused with music. He had a predilection for the music of Earth in the 1960s. He was killed by Davros' new strain of Daleks. (6Z)

DN6
The insecticide developed by Smithers for Forester's company. (J)

d'ARGENSON
An aristocrat, encountered by the First Doctor using Jules Renan's escape route. He was killed by revolutionary soldiers. (H)

d'ARTAGNAN
Dumas' fictional hero summoned by the Second Doctor to help in the battle against the Master of the Land of Fiction's villains. (UU)

da VINCI, Leonardo
The 15th century Italian scientist and painter whom the Doctor implies he has met (5H) and has certainly met the Monk. (S)

DAEMONS
The beings originating from Demos which visited the Earth from time to time, influencing its history by inspiring the Greek civilisation, the Renaissance, the Industrial Revolution and causing part of the destruction of Atlantis. The power of the last of these beings, Azal, was invoked by the Master, who coveted it for himself. (JJJ)

DAFFODILS
450,000 plastic daffodils distributed by Autons as a false publicity gimmick had in fact a deadly asphyxiating device hidden within them. They were invented by the

Master, as part of the plan for the second Nestene attempted invasion of Earth. (EEE)

DAKO
One of the resistance fighters encountered by the First Doctor on Xeros. (Q)

DALE, Professor
A leading member of the Peace Party of Earth in 2540. He was a political prisoner in the penal colony on the Moon and attempted to escape from there along with the Third Doctor. (QQQ)

DALEKANIUM
The name given to the metal of the casing of the Daleks' travel machines by Earthmen. (K, KKK)

DALEKS
The Daleks are the ultimate mutation of the Kaled (or Dal, in an earlier form) people on the planet Skaro. The genetic engineering of their foremost scientist, Davros, produced an unbearably hideous creature rarely glimpsed (B, EE, 4E, 5J, 6P) and devoid of all human feeling and compassion. It is encased in a travel machine, also designed by Davros, to permit mobility. The mutation inside the metal casing is able to see by means of a lens on the end of an eye-stalk, and possesses a probe on the end of a retractable arm. It is equipped with a weapon which is capable of a range of frequency of intensity from disabling (B, SSS) to killing, as seen in all of the Doctor's encounters with the Daleks save one (XXX), at which

moment all have a propensity for ejaculating 'Exterminate' in their grating monosyllabic voice-tones. The probe is interchangeable with other devices such as a grappling claw, a seismic recorder and an electrode unit (R, V). Inside the upper part of the casing, which can be opened, there is a distress signal which is triggered should the Dalek become immobilised. (SSS)

The colour of most Dalek casings is grey with the exception of those that Davros created on Necros, which are white (6Z) and those ranking higher than the majority, which are black. Although at one time the Daleks had an Emperor (LL) they are loyal to the Dalek Supreme, whose casing has been shown as gold (KKK) or gold and black (SSS). As they developed their technology the Daleks emulated the TARDIS and devised their own time machine (R); they also discovered how to subjugate humanoid life forms and control them. (K, LL, 6P)

The Doctor first encountered them in their city on Skaro after their war with the Thals, the other major inhabitants of the planet. At first they were dependent upon static electricity in order to move (B), but by the time he next came across them, on Earth in 2164, they had developed travel discs and saucers capable of interplanetary travel. (K)

The Daleks set about mastering time travel and they chased the Doctor and his companions through time and space until their squad was annihilated in battle with the Mechanoids on the planet Mechanus (R); by then they had also developed their own travel capacity and had dispensed with the travel discs.

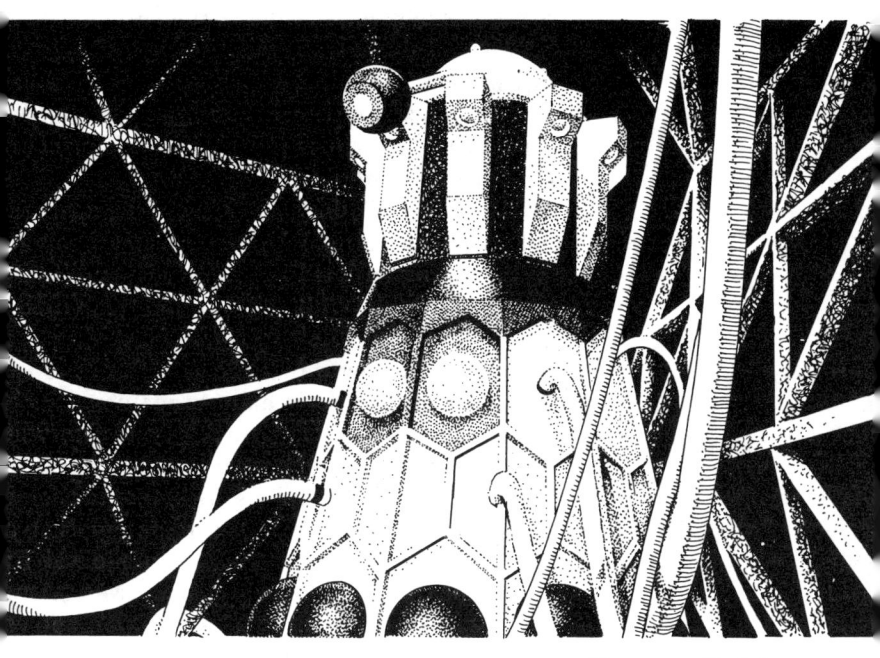

Emperor Dalek

The Doctor met up with them in 4000 on the planet Kembel where he helped to thwart their alliance with other star systems. Their plans to conquer the entire universe failed and their own weapon, the Time Destructor, was used against them.

Shortly after his first regeneration the Doctor helped defeat a squadron menacing the Earth Colony on Vulcan in 2030 (EE) and was later kidnapped and forced to help distil the Dalek factor for his foes before civil war broke out on Skaro. (LL)

In his third incarnation the Doctor was caught in a time paradox when history was changed by human resistance fighters, who travelled from the 22nd century to prevent a second invasion of Earth by the Daleks

(KKK). Next the Master in the employ of the metallic monstrosities tried unsuccessfully to set Earth and Draconia in direct opposition to each other (QQQ). The Doctor went on to tackle the Dalek forces massed on Spiridon, with the unexpected aid of a suicide squad of Thal astronauts (SSS). The Daleks had been seeking the power of invisibility from the native population.

The planet Exxilon, through the beacon atop its major city deprived both the TARDIS of motive-power and the Dalek weapons of fire-power (XXX) in his next match with the Daleks. Then the Fourth Doctor was despatched to Skaro at the birth of the Dalek creatures with instructions from the Time Lords to abort or avert their development. (4E)

The Daleks fought a war with the Movellans and finding both sides at an impasse sought out their creator, buried on Skaro, to help them to break it (5J). However, they were unsuccessful and the Movellans hid some nerve gas in Earth's past. The Daleks coveted this gas to aid in achieving their aspirations of invading Gallifrey (6P) but were hampered by the actions of the Fifth Doctor.

Davros escaped to the planet Necros where he developed a new strain of Dalek, which he encased in white travel machines. Two of his assistants, abetted by the Sixth Doctor, called in the rulers of Skaro who destroyed the white Daleks and took their creator back to his home planet to face the Dalek Supreme.

Not all Dalek battles have involved the Doctor but they have attracted the attention of the Time Lords (4E) and at least one

Dalek was transported to the Death Zone on Gallifrey to challenge any would-be player of the Game of Rassilon. (6K)

King Dalios

DALIOS
The king of Atlantis who was deposed by the Master in his quest for the Crystal of Kronos and imprisoned in his own dungeon, where he died. (OOO)

DALY FAMILY
Major Daly and his daughter Claire were passengers on the S.S. Bernice which was kidnapped and stored in a time-loop in the miniscope brought to Inter-Minor by the Lurman Vorg and Shirna. (PPP)

DAMON
The assistant to Professor Zaroff. (GG)

DAMON
The assistant to Talon in the main computer room in the Capitol on Gallifrey and a friend of the Doctor. (6E)

DAMNONIUM
The district in which Boscombe Moor is located. (5C)

DANIEL
A pirate on Samuel Pike's ship. He was killed by Josiah Blake's men. (CC)

DANIELS, Jim
An astronaut on Recovery 6, accidentally killed by alien ambassadors on Mars. (CC)

THE DARK TOWER
The Dark Tower is in the centre of the Death Zone on Gallifrey and houses the Tomb of Rassilon. (6K)

DARKIE
A dog belonging to Sam and Meg Seeley. (AAA)

DARP
A planet visited by Tryst's expedition. (5K)

DARRIUS
A scientist to whom Arbitan entrusted the safekeeping of one of the micro-circuit keys to the 'Conscience of Marinus'. He was strangled by one of the vines in the Screaming Jungle. (E)

DASK
The Chief Fixer of the sandminer on which the TARDIS materialised. He was disposed of by Taren Capel who then substituted himself for him aboard the craft. (4R)

DASSUK
One of the Guardians on the Ark who helped Steven to bring about peace with the Monoids on the First Doctor's second visit there. (X)

DASTARI, Joinson
A pioneer of genetic engineering and former friend of the Doctor who helped Stike and Chessene in their quest to mobilise the Kartz-Reimer time module before being shot by the latter. (6W)

DAVEY, Captain
An Eternal who took part in the race for Enlightenment in a 19th century clipper, which was sabotaged by Wrack. (6H)

DAVID
One of the sewer surveyors taken prisoner and cybernised by the Cybermen. (6T)

DAVIDSON, Ann
A girl who had been substituted by one of *The Faceless Ones* and posed as a stewardess working for Chameleon Tours. (KK)

DAVIES, Dave
A miner at the Llanfairfach colliery. (TTT)

DAVIS

A seismology technician at Brittanicus base in 3000. He was killed in an avalanche of snow. (OO)

DAVIS

A junior technician at the Atomic Research Centre on Wenley Moor. He was killed in a pot-holing accident. (BBB)

DAVIS, Police Constable

The policeman who investigated the shrinking of his colleague, P.C. Seagrave. (5V)

DAVROS

The crippled Kaled scientist who created the Daleks and was entombed in the Bunker

Davros And The Daleks

(4E). His life support system kept him alive until he was revived in an attempt by his creations to break the stalemate of the Dalek–Movellan war (5J). His efforts were defeated and he was transported to Earth and kept in cryogenic suspension for 90 years before he was revived as part of the Dalek plan to invade Gallifrey (6P). He fled to Necros where he developed a new strain of Dalek and set about revenging himself on the Doctor. His new Daleks were defeated by a patrol from Skaro and he was taken there to face trial before the Dalek Supreme, his hand having been injured by a shot from Bostock's gun in the skirmish. (6Z)

DAWSON, Miss

One of the staff at the Atomic Research Centre on Wenley Moor; the assistant and particular friend to John Quinn, who was aware of his contact with the Silurians. (BBB)

DAWSON, Mollie

The maid in Theodore Maxtible's house. (LL)

DAXTAR

The director of the Experimental Station where Bret Vyon landed Mavic Chen's spaceship. He was a traitor and was shot by Vyon. (V)

de BERGERAC, Cyrano

The fictional hero summoned by the Second Doctor to help in the battle against the

Master of the Land of Fiction's villains. (UU)

de COLIGNY, Gaspard

The Protestant Admiral in France in 1572 who sought Dutch support for a war with the Catholics as the 'Sea Beggar'. He was wounded in an attempted assassination by Bondot in the pay of the Marshal of France and the Queen Mother and was subsequently slaughtered in the St Bartholomew's Eve Massacre. (W)

de HAAN

A member of Salamar's crew who was destroyed on Zeta-Minor by the anti-matter creature. (4H)

de LACY, Sir Geoffrey

The cousin of Ranulf Fitzwilliam. He was shot with a crossbow bolt on the orders of the Master. (6J)

de LEVIS, Gaston

The Vicomte de Lerans and a leading Huguenot in France in 1572. (W)

de MARUN, Reynier

A crusader in the service of Richard the Lionheart. He was shot, with an arrow, by the Saracens. (P)

de MEDICI, Catherine

The Queen Mother of France in 1572 and main instigator of the Saint Bartholomew's Eve Massacre on August 24th that year. (W)

Catherine de Medici

de SAUX-TAVANNES, Gaspard
The Marshal of France in 1572. (W)

de TORNEBU, William
A crusader in the service of Richard the Lionheart. He was wounded, with an arrow, by the Saracens. (P)

de VRIES, Leonard
The leader of the British Institute of Druidic Studies. He was crushed by one of the Ogri. (5C)

DE-MAT GUN
The ultimate weapon of the Time Lords, knowledge of which was forbidden by a decree of Rassilon. Rodan built one under hypnosis, the knowledge gleaned from the Matrix by the Fourth Doctor being passed on to her by K-9. He used it to defeat Stor. (4Z)

DEATH UNDER THE RED CLOTH
A military procedure on Androzani Major. Guilty prisoners were shot whilst covered with a red cloth after which the bodies were taken to the Field Cremation Unit and the ashes from them were then wrapped in the red cloth and disposed of as the prisoners had directed before execution. Chellak proposed to have the Fifth Doctor and Peri eliminated in this ritual. (6R)

DEATH ZONE
A closed-off, forbidden area of Gallifrey

sealed behind an impenetrable forcefield in which the Black Tower, the tomb of Rassilon, is located. (6K)

DEAUVILLE
The French port from which Palmerdale's yacht was returning before it was wrecked on Fang Rock. (4V)

DECIDERS
The three leaders of the starliner community on Alzarius, the chief of whom was the only person permitted to view the System Files. (5R)

DEEDRIX
A Savant, one of the scientific and technical caste on the planet Tigella. (5Q)

DEERING, William
William Deering & Son was the company from which Edward Waterfield purchased a deed box in 1866 to sell in his Chelsea antique shop in 1966 on the orders of the Daleks. (LL)

DEFLECTION BARRIER
A forcefield placed around the home of Marcus Scarman by Sutekh. (4G)

DELL
An Alzarian scientist who existed fifty years before the Fourth Doctor's visit there. (5R)

DELLA
One of the members of Tryst's expedition who aided the Fourth Doctor. (5K)

DELOS
The Greek who befriended Ian when they were made galley-slaves on a Roman vessel. (M)

DELPHON
A planet where the inhabitants communicate by moving their eyebrows, mentioned by the Third Doctor. (AAA)

DELTA MAGNA
An Earth colony and the original home of the Swampies until they were deported to Delta Three. (5E)

DELTA REPAIR KIT
The tool-kit aboard the sandminer on which the TARDIS materialised. (4P)

DELTA THREE
One of the moons of Delta Magna where Kroll had swallowed the fifth segment of the Key to Time. (5E)

DELTA WAVE AUGMENTOR
A device which the Fifth Doctor concocted from his Sonic Screwdriver to induce Nyssa to sleep and rid herself of her mild mental disorientation. (5Y)

DEMETER SEEDS
A discovery of Professor Sarah Lasky and her team and named by one of them, Bruchner, after the Greek goddess. (7C)

DEMNOS
A Roman cult which all but died out in the 3rd century but was resurrected in the province of San Martino in 15th century Italy and utilised for its own purposes by the Mandragora Helix. (4M)

DEMOS
The planet, sixty thousand light years away from Earth, from which the Daemons originate. (JJJ)

DENES
The Zone Controller of the Central European Zone in 2017. He was placed under house arrest by Salamander and shot by a captain of his security staff during a rescue attempt by Jamie, Victoria and Astrid Ferrier. (PP)

DENT, Captain
The ruthless commander of the IMC squad on Uxarius in 2972 who attempted to dispose of the colonists there. (HHH)

DEONS
The caste on Tigella which worshipped Ti and his 'gift', the Dodecahedron. (5Q)

DERVISH
A reluctant space pirate over whom his

leader, Caven, had a hold. He was killed when the spaceship in which he was fleeing from Lobos exploded under attack by Warne. (YY)

des PREAUX, William
The crusader in the service of Richard the Lionheart who impersonated his monarch and was taken prisoner by El Akir, thus allowing his lord to escape. (P)

DESPERUS
A prison planet in 4000 from which Kirksen escaped. (V)

DET-SEN MONASTERY
The lamasery in Tibet which came under attack from the Yeti in 1928, when its Master, Padmasambvha, was possessed by the Great Intelligence. On a previous visit in 1630 the Doctor had been entrusted with the monastery's holy Ghanta – a Tibetan bell – for sakekeeping. (NN)

DEVA-LOKA
The planet on which the Kinda tribe dwell, known to the Expeditionary Team sent there, under the command of Sanders, as S14. (5Y)

DEVESHAM
The village duplicated on Oseidon by the Kraals and where UNIT was temporarily based at a Space Defence Station. (4J)

DEVIL'S END
The village where the Master (posing as the

local vicar, Magister) invoked the power of Azal, the last of the Daemons who visited Earth and helped shape its history, whose spaceship was buried within the barrow known as the Devil's Hump. (JJJ)

DEVIL'S PUNCHBOWL
The small loch just outside the village of Tulloch. (4F)

DEXETER
The head of the science unit on the Terradonian starliner. He was strangled by a marsh-child upon whom he had been experimenting. (5R)

DIANANE
The atmosphere in which Usurians live; it is poisonous to Earthmen. (4W)

DIBBER
The somewhat dim partner-in-crime of Sabalom Glitz from the planet Salostophus. (7A)

DIDIUS
A Roman slave-trader who captured Barbara and Ian. (M)

DIDO
A planet visited before by the First Doctor and where Bennett had attempted the genocide of its inhabitants and from where Vicki joined the crew of the TARDIS, leaving behind the crashed Earth spaceship in which she and Bennett arrived there. (L)

DIGBY, Raymond
The male nurse employed by the Cranleigh family in 1925. He was strangled by the deranged George Cranleigh. (6A)

DILL, Morton
The tourist from Alabama encountered by the First Doctor atop the Empire State Building during his flight from the Daleks. (R)

DINGLE, Sir Maxwell
A bio-physicist and one of the scientists working at the research centre where the Third Doctor first met Sarah-Jane. (UUU)

DIOMEDES
The name Vicki gave to Steven to cover his true identity during their visit to Troy. (U)

DIPLOS
A planet in the Tau Ceti star system from which the criminal Cessair originated. (5C)

Morton Dill

DISINTEGRATOR GUN
The weapon built by the SRS from the plans stolen from the Ministry of Defence Weaponry Research Centre by Jeremiah Kettlewell's robot. (4A)

DISTRONIC TOXAEMIA
A condition, resulting from exposure to radiation from distronic explosives, to which possibility Sarah-Jane was subjected when forced to load the Thal rocket on Skaro. (4E)

DOBSON
A senior computer technician at Space Control Centre and assistant to Bruno Taltalian. (CC)

THE DOCTOR
See in-depth study in the last volume of this encyclopedia.

DODECAHEDRON
The dodecahedron was developed by the leading energy-scientists on Zolpha-Thura as a power source. Other scientists realised its potential as a weapon, which was eventually designed by Meglos. When Zolpha-Thura split into two warring factions all inhabitants were wiped out bar Meglos and the leader of the peace party who fled to Tigella, where he died in a crash landing, taking the Dodecahedron with him. It was found and worshipped by the Deons but eventually used as a power source again by the Savants. Meglos re-appropriated it ten thousand years later and returned it to Zolpha-Thura where it was destroyed when Grugger misguidedly blew up that planet. (5Q)

DODO
Having witnessed an accident on Wimbledon Common, Dorothea Chaplet, or Dodo for short, ran to the TARDIS to summon help, naturally thinking it to be an actual police box. The fact that she might have been a descendant of Anne Chaplette, whom the First Doctor and Steven had just left in 16th century France and that she somewhat re-

Dodo

sembled Susan, coupled with the imminent arrival of some policemen, caused the Doctor to momentarily forget himself and he dematerialised the ship with her still on board.

Dodo's principal joy in travelling with the Doctor lay not in experiencing untold wonders of the universe or meeting someone from history or marvelling at feats of engineering and technology beyond a schoolgirl's wildest dreams, indeed she seemed to take the console room in her stride when she first came through the doors of the TARDIS (W). She seemed to gain the greatest pleasure in sampling the contents of the Doctor's vast wardrobe, viz. the Crusader uniform (X), the 'modern miss' T-shirt, fish-net tights and Dylan cap (Y) and cowgirl outfit (Z). Once she returned to her own time some six journeys later, she was only too happy to stay. She returned to her aunt (since she was an orphan) after the effects of WOTAN's brain-washing wore off (BB). Indeed, she did not take her leave of the Doctor personally, but sent a message via Ben and Polly, a fact which rather hurt her would-be mentor and on which he remarked before he dematerialised his ship en route for 17th century Cornwall.

DOJJEN
A snakedancer and former Federator of Manussa who helped the Fifth Doctor destroy the Mara there. (6D)

DOLAND
One of the assistants of Sarah Lasky. He was a murderer who plotted to exploit the Vervoids and was subsequently killed by them. (7C)

THE DOME
A white-walled prefabricated building on Deva-Loka; the headquarters of the members of the Expeditionary Team sent there under the command of Sanders. (5Y)

THE DOMINATORS
A callous war-loving race, two of whom, Rago and Toba, made an emergency landing on the Island of Death on Dulkis and proceeded to turn the planet into radio-active

The Second Doctor And Dominator Toba

fuel for their fleet. They, and their robot servants, the Quarks, were destroyed when the Second Doctor secreted their own atomic seed device back aboard their vessel, which they then detonated. (TT)

DORAN
One of the Engineers to Adrasta whom she had flung into the Pit where he was smothered by Erato. (5G)

DORF
The equerry of the warlord Yrcanos from Konval on Thordon who was transmuted by Crozier into the Lukoser on Thorus Beta, where he was subsequently killed. (7B)

DORIS

A former girlfriend of the Brigadier's who presented him with a watch on the occasion when they spent a weekend in Brighton. (ZZZ)

DORTMUN

The crippled scientist who led the resistance against the Daleks in 2164. He sacrificed himself to be killed by a Dalek patrol in order to give Barbara and Jenny time to escape from it. (K)

DOUBLES

The exact resemblance of a humanoid lifeform. During their adventures the Doctor and/or his companions have encountered doubles on Androzani Minor (6R), Argolis (5N), asteroid K.4067 (4T), Earth (W, KK, PP, GGG, KKK, 4F, 4J, 6A, 6C, 6E), Gallifrey (6K), Mechanus (R), Sarn (6Q), Tara (5D), Tigella (5P), Xeros (Q) and Zolpha-Thura (5P) and also in space (5Z), on the Shadow's planet of evil (5F) and on an alternate Earth. (DDD)

DRACONIA

A planet which despite technical advances equal to those of Earth in 2540 had remained a monarchy. The Doctor visited the planet 500 years before this, in the time of its fifteenth emperor and helped the Draconians to overcome a space plague, a deed for which he was made an honorary nobleman of the planet. This stood him in good stead on his second visit to the planet when he was able to expose the Master's plot to the current

Draconians

emperor – to set it and Earth at war by the use of his hypno-sound device and the Ogrons. Draconians are very tall with dragon-like features, scaly skin and tapering ears. (QQQ)

DRAGA, Field Guard
The guard who served the Eight-Legs who was attacked by Arak, for which deed Queen Huath ordered the latter's arrest. (ZZZ)

DRAGONS
An Earth slang term for Draconians in 2540. (QQQ)

DRAHVINS
A cloned species of female warriors encountered by the First Doctor in Galaxy Four. (T)

DRAITH, Exmon
The First Decider on Alzarius at the time of the Fourth Doctor's visit there. He was drowned shortly after seeking out Adric at Mistfall. (5R)

DRAK
A Jacondan who although serving Mestor was sympathetic to the Doctor's views and was therefore killed by his master by having his mind burned out. (6S)

DRAKE, Sir Francis
The Elizabethan sea captain whom the Doctor mentions he has met. (5W)

DRASHIGS
Dragon-like carnivorous creatures kidnapped from one of the moons of the planet Grundel and stored in a time-loop in the miniscope brought to Inter-Minor by the Lurman Vorg and Shirna (PPP). These creatures so terrified Jo that she imagined that she saw them again when under the influence of the Master's hypno-sound device (QQQ). Professor Hubert Clegg was able to sense that the sonic screwdriver had been used against them when he examined it, as images of the creatures appeared on the screen of the Third Doctor's IRIS machine. (ZZZ)

Drashig And The Third Doctor

DRATHRO
An L-3 robot from the constellation of Andromeda who, known as the Immortal, ruled Ravolox. It was destroyed when it was caught in its own black light explosion. (7A)

DRAVIDIUS
The planet from which Condo was deported. (4K)

DRAX
A renegade Time Lord who attended the Academy on Gallifrey at the same time as the Doctor. He built the computer, Mentalis, and helped the Fourth Doctor frustrate the plans of the Shadow. (5F)

DREW
One of the guards at the castle where the Master was confined under Colonel Trenchard's supervision. (LLL)

DRISCOLL
A technician at the Nunton Experimental Complex. He was destroyed in an 'unexplosion' there, which he triggered whilst his will was dominated by Eldrad. (4N)

DRONE
A robot on the leper ship programmed to keep the corridors on it clear of obstruction. (6G)

du PONT
One of the conditioned French participants in the *War Games* in the World War I zone. (ZZ)

DUCAT, Amelia
The eccentric painter whose aid was enlisted by the World Ecology Bureau at the time of the attempted invasion of Earth by the Krynoid. (4L)

DUFFY, Sergeant
One of the army personnel who held the Third Doctor and Sarah-Jane, having mistaken them for looters. (WWW)

DUGDALE
The owner of the Hall of Mirrors in the market place on Manussa. (6D)

DUGEEN
The radar operator and member of the Sons of Earth at the refinery on Delta Three. He was shot by his superior, Thawn. (5E)

DUGGAN
A private detective employed by a group of art dealers to investigate the motives and movements of Count Scarlioni. (5H)

DUGGAN, Bill
An amateur botanist and the Security Officer on the *Wheel in Space*. He was shot by Leo Ryan. (SS)

DUKKHA
The representation of the Mara which Tegan dreamed about when she fell asleep under the wind-chimes on Deva-Loka. (5Y)

DULKIS
The planet whose peace-loving people were threatened by the Dominators. 170 years earlier it had been devastated by a great war as a result of which the manufacture of weapons was forbidden by its Second Council. When he helped to destroy the Dominators there it was the Doctor's second visit to the planet. (TT)

DUNBAR, Richard
The deputy to Sir Colin Thackeray at the World Ecology Bureau who sold information to Harrison Chase. He was killed by a Krynoid. (4L)

DUNE
The technician on the Ark in Space used as the host for the Wirrn eggs by the invading Queen. (4C)

DURALINIUM
The mineral on Uxarius for which IMC were anxious to mine (HHH) and the metal of which the door of the weapons arsenal on Peladon was made. (YYY)

DUVAL, Simon
The personal secretary to Gaspard de Saux-Tavannes. (W)

DWARF STAR ALLOY
An over-heavy metal resulting from a technique which utilises some of the properties of a dwarf star (a burnt-out and collapsed sun). Korvik's ship was constructed from it. (5S)

DYMOND
The pilot of the Hecate and an interplanetary smuggler of vraxoin; he was caught by Landing Officer Costa with the assistance of the Fourth Doctor. (5K)

DYNASTRENE
The metal from which the safe of Joseph Chambers was made. (4A)

DYNATROPE
The spacecraft belonging to the Krotons made of tellurium. It was destroyed by Jamie and Beta with sulphuric acid. (WW)

Dyoni

DYONI
One of the Thal group encountered by the First Doctor on his original trip to Skaro. She was promised in marriage to Alydon. (B)

DYRANIUM
The metal of which the air duct grilles on Space Station Nerva were made. (4C)

DYSON, Ernest John
The British Supervising Engineer at Snowcap base in Antarctica in 1986. (DD)

ARTISTE APPENDIX

Abbot of Amboise	William Hartnell
Abbott, Tom	David Purcell
Ablif	Ray Callaghan
Abu	Terence Brown
Achilles	Cavan Kendall
Acomat	Philip Voss
Adam	Brian Badcoe
Corporal Adams	Max Faulkner
Adrasta	Myra Frances
Adric	Matthew Waterhouse
Agamemnon	Francis de Wolff
Agella	Suzanne Danielle
Aggedor	Nick Hobbs
Ahmed	Vik Tablian
Ainu	Tim Munro
Senator Alcott	Tommy Duggan
Aldo	Freddie Earlle
Allen	Stanley McGeagh
Alpha Centauri	Stuart Fell (body)
	Ysanne Churchman (voice)
Altos	Robin Phillips
Alydon	John Lee
Amazonia	Wendy Danvers
Ambril	John Carson
Amyand	James Bate
Anat	Anna Barry
Anatta	Anna Wing
Andor	Victor Lucas
Andred	Chris Tranchell
Jim Andrews	Peter Cellier
John Andrews	Ian Marter
Anicca	Roger Milner
Anita	Carmen Gomez
Anithon	Hugh Hayes
Ankh	Frank Jarvis
Antodus	Marcus Hammond
Anton	Henry Stamper

Ara	Catherine Howe
Arak (ZZZ)	Gareth Hunt
Arak (6V)	Stephen Yardley
Aram	Christine Kavanagh
Doña Arana	Aimee Delamain
Arbitan	George Coulouris
Colonel Archer	Del Henney
The Archimandrite	Cyril Shaps
Arcturus	Murphy Grumbar (body)
	Terry Bale (voice)
Arden	George Waring
Areta	Geraldine Alexander
Aris	Adrian Mills
Staff Sergeant Arnold	Jack Woolgar
Ascaris	Barry Jackson
Mary Ashe	Helen Worth
Robert Ashe	John Ringham
Ashton	Patrick O'Connell
Princess Astra	Lalla Ward
Colonel Attwood	Guy Middleton
Atza	Sam Howard
Aukon	Emrys James
Autloc	Keith Pyott
Avon	Robert Sidaway
Axon boy	John Hicks
Axon girl	Debbie Lee London
Axon man	Bernard Holley
Axon woman	Patricia Gordeno
Axus	Richard Ireson
Aydan	Martin Cort
Azal	Stephen Thorne
Azaxyr	Alan Bennion
Azmael	Maurice Denham
Baccu	Ian Frost
Francis Bacon	Roger Hammond
Baker	Richard McNeff
Major Baker	Norman Jones
Balan	Johnson Bayley

Balaton	Ralph Michael
Balazar	Adam Blackwood
Baldwin	Tony McEwan
Bane	Anne Clements
Barbara	Jacqueline Hill
Barclay	Terry Walsh
Tom Barclay	David Dodimead
Barnes	Christopher Burgess
Barney	Graham Armitage
George Barnham	Neil McCarthy
Major Barrington	Terence Bayler
Tim Bass	William Ilkley
Bates	Michael Attwell
Bax	Graham Cull
Chief Baxter	Richard Mayes
Ruth Baxter	Barbara Ward
The Beatles	Themselves
Doctor Beavis	Henry McCarthy
Corporal Bell	Fernanda Marlowe
Bellal	Arnold Yarrow
Ben	Michael Craze
Ben (4V)	Ralph Watson
Ben Daheer	Reg Pritchard
Benik	Milton Johns
Bennett	Ray Barrett
Jarvis Bennett	Michael Turner
Roger Benoit	Andre Maranne
Corporal/Sergeant/ RSM Benton	John Levene
Major Beresford	John Acheson
Berger	June Bland
Beta (WW)	James Cairncross
Bettan	Harriet Philpin
Bigon	Philip Locke
Bill	Stephen Churchett
Andrew Bilton	Michael Cashman
Binro	Timothy Bateson
Biroc	David Weston
Bisham	David Rowlands

Black Guardian	Valentine Dyall
Blackbeard	Gerry Wain
Captain Blade	Donald Pickering
Corporal Blake	Richardson Morgan
Josiah Blake	John Ringham
Bloodaxe	John J Carney
Blor	Michael Crane
Jane Blythe	June Murphy
Boaz	Scott Fredericks
Bok	Stanley Mason
Bor	Peter Benson
The Borad	Robert Ashby
Borg	Brian Croucher
Borkar	James Hall
Bors	Dallas Cavell
Borusa	Angus Mackay (4P)
	John Arnatt (4Z)
	Leonard Sachs (6E)
	Philip Latham (6K)
Bostock	John Ogwen
Oscar Botcherby	James Saxon
Bovem	Alan Gerrard
Leading Telegraphist Bowman	Alec Wallis
Bragen	Bernard Archard
Major Branwell	Clifford Earl
Braun	Terence Brook
Brazen	Peter Gilmore
Brent	Ric Felgate
Professor Brett	John Harvey
Brewster	Brian Hawksley
Briggs	Beryl Reid
Benjamin Briggs	David Blake Kelly
Samantha Briggs	Pauline Collins
Brock	John Collin
Broken Tooth	David Rodigan
John Bromley	Ian Fairbairn
Congressman Brook	Ramsay Williams
Brotadac	Frederick Treves

Broton — John Woodnutt
Brownrose — Dermot Tuohy
Donald Bruce — Colin Douglas
Bruchner — David Allister
Brunner — Peter Robert Scott
Corporal Bryson — Colin Bell
Jennifer Buckingham — Jane Sherwin
Bulic — Nigel Humphreys
Joseph Buller — Alan Butler
Burns — Christopher Matthews
Sergeant-Major Burns — Esmond Webb
Butler — Martin Javis

The Caber — Robert Russell
Sergeant Calder — Philip McGough
Caldwell — Bernard Kay
Calib — Leslie Schofield
Jim Callum — Clive Merrison
Cameca — Margot van der Burgh
Victor Camford — Raymond Westwell
Camilla — Rachel Davies
David Campbell — Peter Fraser
Taren Capel — David Bailie
The Captain — Bruce Purchase
Caris — Colette Gleeson
Mick Carney — John Garvin
General Carrington — John Abineri
Carson — Christopher Whittingham
Jeremy Carstairs — David Savile
Carter (6B) — Mark Straker
Doctor Carter — Rex Robinson
Enrico Casali — Donald Sumpter
Casey — Chris Cannon
Cass (4R) — Tariq Unus
Cassandra — Frances White
Maurice Caven — Dudley Foster
Celation — Terence Woodfield
Cessair — Susan Engel
Chal — Ewen Solon

Chameleons	Robin Dawson
	Barry Dupre
	Pat Leclere
	Ron Pearce
Corporal Champion	James Haswell
Will Chandler	Keith Jayne
Ken Chang	Peter Laird
Channing	Hugh Burden
Anne Chaplette	Annette Robertson
Charles	Anthony Calf
Charles IX	Barry Justice
Charlie (Z)	David Graham
Charlie (HH)	Robin Scott
Charlie (FFF)	David Calderisi
Charlie (HHH)	John Scott Martin
Charlie (JJJ – village)	John Scott Martin
Charlie (JJJ – BBC3)	Robin Squire
Harrison Chase	Tony Beckley
Chedaki	Roy Skelton
Chela	Johnathon Morris
General Chellak	Martin Cochrane
Mavic Chen	Kevin Stoney
Chenchu	Jimmy Gardner
Cheng Teik	Francis Batsoni
Cherub	George A Cooper
Chessene	Jacqueline Pearce
Doctor Chester	Ian Fairbairn
Chin Lee	Pik-Sen Lim
Horatio Chinn	Peter Bathurst
Cho-je	Kevin Lindsay
Harold Chorley	Jon Rollason
Chub	Rob Edwards
Chumblies	Jimmy Kaye
	Angelo Muscat
	Pepi Poupee
	Tommy Reynolds
	William Sheaver
Milo Clancey	Gordon Gostelow
Billy Clanton	David Cole

Ike Clanton	William Hurndell
Pa Clanton	Reed de Rouen
Phineas Clanton	Maurice Good
Clara the Clown	Carmen Silvera
Alan Clark	Declan Mulholland
Hubert Clegg	Cyril Shaps
Ernie Clements	George Tovey
Clent	Peter Barkworth
Angela Clifford	Judith Byfield
Corporal Cockerill	Maurice O'Connell
Codal	Tim Preece
Léon Colbert	Edward Brayshaw
Roger Colbert	Chris Tranchell
Adam Colby	Edward Arthur
Colin	Adam Verney
The Collector	Henry Woolf
Collier	Clive Kneller
Collins	Michael Bilton
Collinson	Robert Robertson
Condo	Colin Fay
The Controller (JJ)	Graham Leaman
The Controller (KKK)	Aubrey Woods
Humphrey Cook	Neville Barber
Coolie	John Wu
Cordo	Roy Macready
Ralph Cornish	Ronald Allen
Gemma Corwyn	Anne Ridler
Marc Cory	Edward de Souza
Costa	Peter Craze
Major Cosworth	Patrick Godfrey
Cotton	Rick James
Jack Craddock	Michael Goldie
Lieutenant Crane	David Valla
Charles Cranleigh	Michael Cochrane
George Cranleigh	Gareth Milne
Margaret Cranleigh	Barbara Murray
Guy Crayford	Milton Johns
Charles Crichton	David Savile
Crito	Derek Murcott

Crozier	Patrick Ryecart
Doctor Cruickshank	Roderick Smith
Cully	Arthur Cox
Police Constable Cummings	Andrew Tourell
Curly	Simon Cain
Curt	Michael Bangerter
General Cutler	Robert Beatty
Terry Cutler	Callen Angelo
Cyber Controller	Michael Kilgariff (MM, 6T)
Cyber Leader	David Banks (6B, 6K, 6T)
	Harry Brookes (DD)
	Gregg Palmer (DD)
	Christopher Robbie (4D)
	Reg Whitehead (DD)
	Sonny Willis (HH)
Cyber Lieutenant	Mark Hardy (6B, 6K)
	Brian Orrell (6T)
Cyber Voices	Peter Halliday (VV)
	Peter Hawkins (DD, HH, MM, SS)
	Roy Skelton (DD, SS)
Cybermen	John Ainley (6T)
	David Bache (6B)
	Norman Bradley (6B)
	Derek Chafer (VV)
	John Clifford (HH)
	Graham Cole (6B)
	Ralph Corrigan (VV)
	Hans de Vries (MM)
	Terence Denville (VV)
	Charles Finch (VV)
	Peter Gates-Fleming (6B)
	Gilbert Gillian (6K)
	Keith Goodman (HH)
	Michael Gordon-Browne (6B)

Pat Gorman (VV, 4D, 6T)
Peter Greene (HH)
John Haines (DD)
Tony Harwood (MM)
John Hogan (MM)
Jerry Holmes (SS)
Steve Ismay (6B)
Emyr Morris Jones (6K)
Melville Jones (4D)
Myrddin Jones (6K)
William Kenton (6K)
Richard Kerley (MM)
Richard King (VV)
John Knott (DD)
Ronald Lee (HH, MM)
John Levene (HH, VV)
Tony Lord (4D)
Thomas Lucy (6T)
Ian Marshall-Fisher (6T)
Richard Naylor (6K)
Barry Noble (HH)
Roy Pearce (ZZ)
Charles Pemberton (MM)
Roger Pope (6T)
Kenneth Seeger (MM)
John Spreadbury (VV)
Gordon Stothard (SS)
Peter Thornton (VV)
Jeff Wayne (6B)
Bruce Wells (DD)
Mark Whincup (6K)
Reg Whitehead (HH, MM)
John Wills (HH)
Lee Woods (6K)

Cyril   Peter Stephens

D.84   Gregory de Polnay
The D.J.   Alexei Sayle
d'Argenson   Neville Smith

d'Artagnan	John Greenwood
Dako	Peter Craze
Professor Dale	Harold Goldblatt
Dalek Operators	Keith Ashley (4E)
	Toby Byrne (6T, 6Z)
	Nick Evans (K)
	Max Faulkner (4E)
	Peter Murphy Grumbar (B, K, Q, LL, KKK, QQQ, SSS, XXX)
	Robert Jewell (B, K, R, V)
	Kevin Manser (B, K, R, V, EE)
	John Scott Martin (R, V, EE, LL, KKK, QQQ, SSS, XXX, 4E, 6K, 6P, 6Z)
	Mike Mungarvan (5J)
	Ricky Newby (KKK)
	Tony Starr (SSS, 6P, 6Z)
	Michael Summerton (B)
	Gerald Taylor (B, K, R, V, EE, LL)
	Cy Town (QQQ, SSS, XXX, 4E, 5J, 6P, 6Z)
	Ken Tyllsen (LL)
Dalek Voices	Oliver Gilbert (KKK)
	David Gooderson (5J)
	David Graham (B, K, R, V)
	Peter Hawkins (B, K, Q, R, V, EE, LL)
	Peter Messaline (KKK)
	Brian Miller (6P)
	Royce Mills (6P, 6Z)
	Roy Skelton (LL, SSS, 4E, 5J, 6K, 6Z)
	Michael Wisher (QQQ, SSS, XXX, 4E)
Dalios	George Cormack
Major Daly	Tenniel Evans
Claire Daly	Jenny McCracken

Damon (GG)	Colin Jeavons
Damon (6E)	Neil Daglish
Darrius	Edmund Warwick
Dassuk	Brian Wright
Joinson Dastari	Laurence Payne
David	Stephen Wale
Ann Davidson	Gilly Fraser
Dave Davies	Talfryn Thomas
Davis (OO)	Peter Diamond
Davis (BBB)	Billy Matthews
Davros	Michael Wisher (4E)
	David Gooderson (5J)
	Terry Molloy (6P, 6Z)
Miss Dawson	Thomasine Heiner
Mollie Dawson	Jo Rowbottom
Daxtar	Roger Avon
Cyrano de Bergerac	David Cannon
Gaspard de Coligny	Leonard Sachs
de Haan	Graham Weston
Geoffrey de Lacy	Michael J Jackson
Gaston de Levis	Eric Thompson
Reynier de Marun	David Anderson
Gaspard de Saux-Tavannes	Andre Morell
William de Tornebu	Bruce Wightman
Leonard de Vries	Nicholas McArdle
Deedrix	Crawford Logan
Della	Jennifer Lonsdale
Delos	Peter Diamond
Denes	George Pravda
Captain Dent	Morris Perry
Dervish	Brian Peck
William des Preaux	John Flint
Dexeter	Tony Calvin
Dibber	Glenn Murphy
Didius	Nicholas Evans
Morton Dill	Peter Purves
Dobson	Juan Moreno
The Doctor	William Hartnell (A–DD, RRR, 6K)

	Patrick Troughton (EE–ZZ, RRR, 6K, 6W)
	Jon Pertwee (AAA–ZZZ, 6K)
	Tom Baker (4A–5V, 6K)
	Peter Davison (5W–6R)
	Colin Baker (6S–7C)
	Richard Hurndall (6K)
Dodo	Jackie Lane
Dojjen	Preston Lockwood
Doland	Malcolm Tierney
Doran	Terry Walsh
Dortmun	Alan Judd
Draconians	Peter Birrel
	Bill Burridge
	Lawrence Davidson
	Ian Frost
	Kevin Maran
	Roy Pattison
	Terry Sartain
	Bill Wilde
	John Woodnutt
Dracula	Malcolm Rogers
Drahvins	Lyn Ashley
	Susanna Carroll
	Marina Martin
Exmon Draith	Leonard Maguire
Drak	Oliver Smith
Drathro	Peter McGuinness (body)
	Roger Brierley (voice)
Drax	Barry Jackson
Drew	Stanley McGeagh
Driscoll	Roy Boyd
du Pont	Peter Craze
Amelia Ducat	Sylvia Coleridge
Sergeant Duffy	Dave Carter
Dugdale	Brian Miller
Dugeen	John Leeson
Duggan	Tom Chadbon
Bill Duggan	Kenneth Watson

Dukkha	Jeffrey Stewart
Richard Dunbar	Kenneth Gilbert
Simon Duval	John Tollinger
Dymond	Geoff Bateman
Dyoni	Virginia Wetherell
Ernest Dyson	Dudley Jones